NINTH EDITION

ILLUSTRATED SERIES™

Computer Concepts

Brief

Computer Concepts

ILLUSTRATED - Ninth Edition

Brief

June Jamrich Parsons / Dan Oja

COURSE TECHNOLOGY
CENGAGE Learning

Australia • Brazil • Japan • Korea • Mexico • Singapore • Spain • United Kingdom • United States

COURSE TECHNOLOGY
CENGAGE Learning·

Computer Concepts—Illustrated Brief, Ninth Edition
June Jamrich Parsons/Dan Oja

Executive Editor: Marjorie Hunt

Associate Acquisitions Editor: Amanda Lyons

Senior Product Manager: Christina Kling Garrett

Associate Product Manager: Kim Klasner

Editorial Assistant: Brandelynn Perry

Technology Product Manager: Jessica Mahoney

Director of Marketing: Elisa Roberts

Marketing Manager: Julie Schuster

Marketing Coordinator: Adrienne Fung

Adapting Author: Rachel Biheller Bunin

Developmental Editor: Pam Conrad

Content Project Manager: Heather Hopkins

Proofreader: Camille Kiobasa

Indexer: BIM Indexing

Photo Researcher: Abby Reip

Web permissions: Kathleen Ryan

Cover Designer: GEX Publishing Services

Cover Artist: GEX Publishing Services

Cover Photographer: ©ARENA Creative/Shutterstock.com; ©Daniele Carotenuto/Shutterstock.com; ©Alan Jeffery/Shutterstock.com; ©MrGarry/Shutterstock.com

Composition: GEX Publishing Services

Manufacturing Planner: Fola Orekoya

For product information and technology assistance, contact us at
Cengage Learning Customer & Sales Support, 1-800-354-9706
For permission to use material from this text or product, submit all requests online at **cengage.com/permissions**
Further permissions questions can be emailed to
permissionrequest@cengage.com

Library of Congress Control Number: 2012930596

ISBN-13: 978-1-133-52616-2
ISBN-10: 1-133-52616-0

Course Technology
20 Channel Center Street
Boston, Massachusetts 02210
USA

Cengage Learning is a leading provider of customized learning solutions with office locations around the globe, including Singapore, the United Kingdom, Australia, Mexico, Brazil, and Japan. Locate your local office at:
international.cengage.com/region

Cengage Learning products are represented in Canada by Nelson Education, Ltd.

To learn more about Course Technology, visit **www.cengage.com/coursetechnology**

To learn more about Cengage Learning, visit **www.cengage.com**

Purchase any of our products at your local college store or at our preferred online store **www.cengagebrain.com**

Printed in the United States of America
1 2 3 4 5 6 15 14 13 12

Brief Contents

Contents

Preface

Welcome to *Computer Concepts Illustrated Brief Ninth Edition!* This book is designed to help students learn and retain the most relevant and essential information about computers and technology in today's digital world. To enhance the teaching and learning experience, you can also bundle this text with CourseMate, our online digital companion site which includes a media-rich eBook, videos and interactive activities for reinforcement, and Engagement Tracker, a first-of-its-kind tool that monitors student engagement in the course.

Designed For All Users

The unique page design of the book makes it a great learning tool for both new and experienced users. Each concept is presented on two facing pages, so students don't have to turn the page to find an illustration or finish a paragraph. Also, because the text is organized in a question and answer format, students can choose to read all of the lesson material or only those questions and answers where they need to "fill in the gaps."

New to This Edition

Here are some highlights of what's new to this edition:

- **CourseMate**—The new CourseMate online companion for this book is packed with media-rich content to engage your students and to help you teach the course! CourseMate includes a **digital version of this book** that students can read and highlight online; brand new **videos** based on the book content that highlight the hot topics of each lesson; **Student Edition Labs** that provide hands-on learning and assessment activities for key concepts; interactive **games**, **flashcards**, and **puzzles** to reinforce what they've learned, and practice test to assess mastery of content. The CourseMate also includes handy Independent Challenge worksheets adapted from the book that students can download, complete, and submit. CourseMate also includes a link to a **weekly podcast** on the hottest technology

Each two-page spread focuses on a single topic.

Introduction briefly explains why the lesson topic is important.

Lesson Objective in each lesson articulates key learning goal of the lesson.

Printers

UNIT B Concepts

Most output is viewed using a display device. This output is called **soft copy**. Sometimes, you want the output on paper. To create printed copy, you use a printer. Printed output is called **hard copy**. You can print hard copy on different media, such as paper, labels, or transparencies. Printers differ in resolution and speed, both of which affect the print quality and price. To find a printer that meets your needs, it is important to understand the different types of printers and their features.

Learning Objective 3:
Describe different types of printers, and explain the advantages and disadvantages of each type

- **What are the most common types of printers in use today?** The most common types of printers in use today are either ink-jet printers or laser printers. Both ink-jet printers and laser printers have features in common. For example, both are available as black and white or color printers. Both have trays for different paper sizes. You can print on 8" × 11" paper, 8" × 14" paper, envelopes, postcards, transparencies, and more. Both types of printers also have drawbacks to consider. For example, cost over the life of the printer, as well as the speed at which the printer produces hard copy.

- **How does an ink-jet printer work?** An **ink-jet printer** has a print head that sprays ink onto paper to form characters and graphics. Ink-jet printers usually use two cartridges: a black ink cartridge and a color cartridge that holds colored inks. See Figure B-9. Most ink-jet printers are small, lightweight, and inexpensive, yet produce very good-quality color output. However, the ink cartridges can be expensive and can add to the overall cost of printing.

FIGURE B-9: An ink jet printer

Color ink cartridges

Paper tray

Black ink cartridge

- **How does a laser printer work?** A **laser printer** uses a technology that produces dots of light on a light-sensitive drum. Instead of ink cartridges, laser printers use **toner** cartridges. See Figure B-10. Toner is the fine powder that is applied to the drum, and then creates the image on the paper. Laser printers are popular for situations that require high-volume output or good-quality printouts. Laser printers are generally more expensive than ink-jet printers.

FIGURE B-10: A laser printer

Toner cartridge

Paper tray

- **What determines the quality of the printed images?** **Printer resolution** determines the quality or sharpness of printed images and text. Resolution is measured by the number of dots printed per linear inch, or **dots per inch (dpi)**. At normal reading distance, a resolution of about 900 dots per inch appears solid to the human eye. At 900 dpi, if you look closely, a dot pattern will be evident. Good-quality printers are rated from 2400 to 4800 dpi. If you want the printed images to have the quality of professionally printed books, use a printer with a resolution of 2400 dpi or higher.

- **How can I know if a printer is fast?** You can look at the pages per minute (ppm) and memory specifications provided by the manufacturer. Printer speed is measured by the number of **pages per minute (ppm)** output. Color printouts typically take longer to print than black-and-white printouts. Pages that contain mostly text tend to print faster than pages that contain graphics. Most printers for personal or small business use are rated from 15 to 30 ppm.
Memory capacity is another factor to consider when evaluating printer speed. Printers often work in the background while you work on other computer tasks. If your printer has lots of

Concepts 32   Computer Hardware

Question & Answer format helps to engage students and make the content relevant.

news hosted by Ken Baldauf of Florida State University. CourseMate comes with **Engagement Tracker**, a unique tool you can use to monitor student engagement. You can use CourseMate all by itself, or bundle it with the book.

- **Updated and Relevant Information**—each page of this book has been completely updated to reflect the most current and relevant information about computers and computing technology. New lessons include Communicating with Digital Devices and Protecting Your Privacy, Data, and Devices. In response to customer feedback, we also made a change to the table of contents; the unit on security is now Unit E, and the unit on Networks and Connecting to the Internet is Unit F.

- **Updated Design**—Our updated design and pedagogy make this edition more engaging for students. Each unit opener page now shows a large photograph of a student using technology related to that unit, and also lists learning objectives and lesson topics for the unit. Each lesson spread now displays the learning objective in a shaded box to help focus the student on the key learning goal for that lesson.

Exercises

Each unit features a wide variety of reinforcement exercises including Key Terms, Unit Review, and Concepts Review multiple choice questions. Other exercises include:

- **Talking Points**—Engage your students in lively discussions by assigning Talking Points, which provide information and discussion questions about computing topics that affect our everyday lives. Examples include Why Recycle Computers? and Who is Reading Your Email?

- **Independent Challenges**—Independent Challenge exercises are guided activities that students complete to reinforce what they have learned in that unit.

- **Buyer's Guide**—this activity lets student organize and record the important information learned in that unit to help them research options and make decisions about purchasing their own computer.

---

memory, you can send many print jobs to the printer. The print jobs will be in the printer's memory and not in your computer's memory. More memory is required to print color images and documents with graphics. You can work more efficiently if your printer has more memory.

- **Can a printer print on both sides of a page in one pass?** Yes, a **duplex printer** can print on both sides of the paper. This environment-friendly option saves paper. However, duplex printing slows down the print process on ink-jet printers because they have to pause to let the ink dry before printing the second side.

- **Does the number of pages I print affect the life of my printer?** **Duty cycle** determines how many pages a printer is able to print in a specified period of time. A printer's duty cycle is usually measured in pages per month. For example, on average, a personal laser printer has a duty cycle of about 3000 pages per month—that means roughly 100 pages per day. However, you wouldn't want to use it to produce 3,000 pages on one day. You can print more pages than the specified duty cycle, but this could shorten the usability of your printer. Also, a printer with a higher duty cycle will have a shorter useful life.

- **How does a printer connect to my computer?** A printer connects to your computer using one of the following connection options: USB port, serial port, parallel port, or network port. Usually a cable is used to connect a printer to a computer. However, a printer can also connect to a computer wirelessly if the printer and computer both have the wireless technology needed to connect.

You can connect a printer directly to your personal computer and use it only with that computer. But, sometimes, you might want to use a printer with more than one computer.

- **How do I use a printer with more than one computer?** If your computers are part of a LAN (local area network), you can share your printer with the other computers. In this situation, each computer on the network sends its print jobs to your computer's printer for output. This allows many computers to share one resource, the printer.

  Another way to configure network printing for multiple users is to purchase a **network-enabled printer** that connects directly to the network, rather than to one of the computers on a network. The network connection can be wired or wireless.

- **Do I need a different printer to print lots of photographs?** Yes, for more professional output, you want to use a **photo printer**. These printers have slower output speeds when compared to ink-jet or laser printers, but they do produce professional-quality images on specialized papers.

- **How do I know which type of printer is best for me?** The type of printer you need depends on several factors. For example: Do you need black and white hard copy or color hard copy Do you often need to print a lot of pages at one time? Are you working with a stand-alone or a networked computer? Do you want a wired or a wireless printer? Once you know the answers to these questions, you will know what type of printer best meets your needs.

Unit B

Options for printing your photos

Do you print a lot of photographs? If so, you should compare the cost of printing the photographs using your printer to the cost of printing the photographs commercially. You can often have digital images printed over the Web using online services, such as Kodak Gallery, Snapfish, or Flickr. The printed photos are then mailed to you. You can also take the digital image files on a disc or flash drive to a store and have the photographs printed there. You can often shop while you wait for your photos. Some stores allow you to upload images to their Web site, where you specify your printing preferences, and then pick up the photos at your local store. Some stores even have self-service stations in the store. See Figure B-11. These printing services usually allow you to edit your digital images, for example, to remove red-eye or to crop an unwanted object out of the image. If you consider the cost of paper and ink to print large quantities of photographs, these services often are more economical. But for occasional use, a photo-printer provides quality images at a reasonable cost.

FIGURE B-11: Self-service photo printing

Courtesy of Hewlett-Packard Company

Computer Hardware | **Concepts 33**

Clues to Use yellow boxes relate the lesson material to real-world situations to provide practical information and context.

Large photos and graphics illustrate the lesson concepts.

CourseMate

Interested in a simple way to *complement* your text and course content with study and practice materials? **CourseMate** brings course concepts to life with interactive learning, study, and exam preparation tools that support the printed textbook. Watch student comprehension soar as your class works with the printed textbook and the CourseMate companion website. CourseMate goes beyond the book to deliver what you need! (CourseMate is sold separately.)

The following interactive activities and tools are included in CourseMate:

• **ebook**—A digital version of this text lets your students read, take notes, and highlight key content using their computer. Students can also search for information they want, and can view or print a PDF of any book page.

• **Video Highlights**—New videos highlighting the key points of each two-page lesson present the content to students the way they learn best.

• **Concepts Review**—Multiple choice questions from the Concepts Review exercises in the book are presented online. Students get immediate feedback on their results.

Video Highlights for each lesson bring book content to life

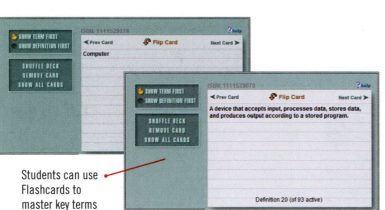

Students can use Flashcards to master key terms

• **Glossary and Flashcards**—Students can study and master key terms for each unit using the online glossary and Flashcard tools.

• **Student Edition Labs**—This collection of animations and hands-on activities help engage students and help them master key computing concepts.

Student Edition Labs feature animations, guided steps, and reinforcement questions to help students learn key concepts

- **Worksheets for Selected Exercises**—Students can download worksheets based on the Independent Challenge and Guide to Buying a Computer exercises. The worksheets contain all the instructions they need to complete the exercises. Students can type their answers directly into form fields on the worksheet and submit to you for grading.

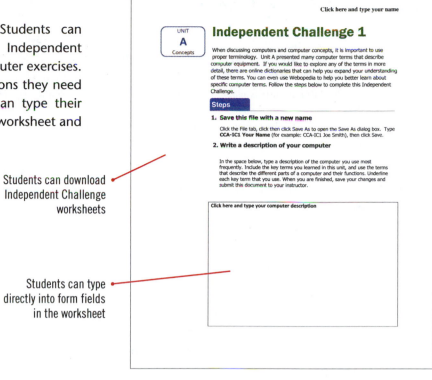

Students can download Independent Challenge worksheets

Students can type directly into form fields in the worksheet

- **Games**—Crossword puzzles and a game let students test their knowledge of key terms and concepts in a fun, engaging way.

- **Practice Tests**—Students can prepare for exams by completing online practice tests on the unit content.

- **CourseCasts**—Keep your class up to date by assigning the CourseCast podcast each week. Hosted by Ken Baldauf of Florida State University, each podcast summarizes the hottest technology news from that week. Assign the CourseCast assignment to make sure that students listen to it! Students can listen on their computer, or they can download it to a mobile device to listen on the go.

- **Engagement Tracker**—Unique tool lets you monitor your students engagement in the course by tracking their usage of each CourseMate activity.

How Do Students Access CourseMate?

Instructions on how to access the CourseMate for this book are in the Getting Started with CourseMate Appendix. Note that students must purchase a CourseMate pin code to access CourseMate.

Instructor Resources

The Instructor Resources CD is Course Technology's way of putting the resources and information needed to teach and learn effectively into your hands. With an integrated array of teaching and learning tools that offer you and your students a broad range of technology-based instructional options, we believe this CD represents the highest quality and most cutting edge resources available to instructors today. Many of these resources are available at www.cengage.com/coursetechnology. The resources available with this book are:

• **Instructor's Manual**—Available as an electronic file, the Instructor's Manual includes detailed lecture topics with teaching tips for each unit.

• **Sample Syllabus**—Prepare and customize your course easily using this sample course outline.

• **PowerPoint Presentations**—Each unit has a corresponding PowerPoint presentation that you can use in lecture, distribute to your students, or customize to suit your course.

• **Figure Files**—The figures in the text are provided on the Instructor Resources CD to help you illustrate key topics or concepts. You can create traditional overhead transparencies by printing the figure files. Or you can create electronic slide shows by using the figures in a presentation program such as PowerPoint.

• **Solutions to Exercises**—Solutions to Exercises contains examples of the work in the end-of-unit material.

• **ExamView**—ExamView is a powerful testing software package that allows you to create and administer printed, computer (LAN-based), and Internet exams. ExamView includes hundreds of questions that correspond to the topics covered in this text, enabling students to generate detailed study guides that include page references for further review. The computer-based and Internet testing components allow students to take exams at their computers, and also saves you time by grading each exam automatically.

Content for Online Learning.

Course Technology has partnered with the leading distance learning solution providers and class-management platforms today. To access this material, visit www.cengage.com/webtutor and search for your title. Instructor resources include the following: video highlights, additional case projects, sample syllabi, PowerPoint presentations, and more. For additional information, please contact your sales representative. For students to access this material, they must have purchased a WebTutor PIN-code specific to this title and your campus platform. The resources for students might include (based on instructor preferences): topic reviews, review questions, practice tests, and more.

COURSECASTS   Learning on the Go. Always Available…Always Relevant.

Our fast-paced world is driven by technology. You know because you are an active participant—always on the go, always keeping up with technological trends, and always learning new ways to embrace technology to power your life. Let CourseCasts, hosted by Ken Baldauf of Florida State University, be your guide into weekly updates in this ever-changing space. These timely, relevant podcasts are produced weekly and are available for download at http://coursecasts.course.com or directly from iTunes (search by CourseCasts). CourseCasts are a perfect solution to getting students (and even instructors) to learn on the go!

Acknowledgements

Author Acknowledgements

We sincerely appreciate all the members of the Illustrated team for contributing their vision, talent, and skills to make this book a reality. Special thanks to Rachel Biheller Bunin for her fast and efficient work as the adapting author, Pamela Conrad for her insights as the developmental editor, Heather Hopkins and Marisa Taylor for their solid work as production editors, Christina Kling Garrett for leading the project.

– June Parsons, Dan Oja, and MediaTechnics for the New Perspectives Series

I am forever grateful to Pam Conrad, the Developmental Editor on this book. Working with Pam is always a wonderful experience. As a personal friend and colleague, she contributes strength, knowledge, and intelligence to the project. My thanks to Marjorie Hunt, Executive Editor, for her encouragement and vision. Gratitude to Christina Kling Garrett, Senior Project Manager, for keeping all the components on track and providing endless support. Special credit to Emily Bunin for the stunning photos that begin each unit. Thanks to Abby Reip for her work collecting the stock photos and keeping it all straight. Thanks to Kathleen Ryan for her work on Web permissions. On the Production side, thanks to Marisa Taylor and Heather Hopkins for a beautiful book. Appreciation to Dan Oja and June Parsons for supporting the project. And finally, special thanks to David, Jennifer, Emily, and Michael.

– Rachel Biheller Bunin, Adapting Author

Advisory Board Acknowledgements

We would like to thank our Advisory Board for their honest feedback and suggestions that helped guide our development decisions for this edition. They are as follows:

Audrey Styer, Morton College

Sheila Sicilia, Onondaga Community College

Michelle Breitigan, Owens Community College

Sherry Lenhart, Terra Community College

Theresa Markovich, Everett Community College of Washington

Computer and Internet Basics

Learning Objectives

1. Define a personal computer and describe computer use in daily life
2. Explain the four basic functions of a computer system
3. Identify the main computer categories
4. Describe digital devices that can be part of a personal computer
5. Define software and give examples of operating systems
6. Define the Internet and explain how to navigate Web pages
7. Explain ways to use the Internet and digital devices to communicate with others
8. Explain how to protect your digital data and devices

LESSON TOPICS

- Computers in Your World
- How Computers Work
- Types of Computers
- Personal Computers
- Computer Software
- The Internet and the Web
- How to Communicate Using Digital Devices
- How to Protect Your Privacy, Data, and Devices

Talking Points: Who is Reading Your Email?

Courtesy of Emily Bunin

Computers in Your World

Whether you realize it or not, you already know a lot about personal computers and other digital devices. You've picked up information from advertisements and magazine articles, from books and movies, from conversations, and perhaps even from using a computer, smartphone, or other digital device. The digital revolution is the reason computers are all around you. See Figure A-1. This lesson helps you start organizing what you know about the digital revolution and computers.

Learning Objective 1:
Define a personal computer and describe computer use in daily life

● **What is the digital revolution and how does it affect me?** The **digital revolution** is an ongoing process of social, political, and economic change brought about by **digital technology**. Digital technology includes digital devices such as computers, portable media players, cameras, mobile phones, smartphones, tablet computers, global positioning systems (GPSs), DVD and CD players, e-book readers, digital voice recorders, and video games. Even cars and appliances, such as microwave ovens, refrigerators, and washing machines, use digital electronics. The digital revolution influences the tools you use to work, play, teach, and govern, especially when you use a computer.

● **What is a computer?** A **computer** is an electronic device that accepts input, processes data, stores data, and produces output as information. If a machine performs these four basic functions, it is a computer.

● **Why would I use a computer?** You might use a computer to access information on the Web, create documents, calculate a budget, change digital photographs, create music, and produce original graphics. Most likely, you will use a computer to communicate with people through the Internet.

● **Do all computers look alike?** No. Computers come in a variety of styles, models, and sizes. The way a computer looks depends on how the computer system is set up and what it will be used for. Usually, when people talk about computers, they are talking about a **personal computer (PC)**. A **computer system** includes hardware, peripheral devices, and software.

● **What is hardware?** **Hardware** refers to the electronic and mechanical parts of the computer. The **system unit** is the box that houses the most important parts of a computer system. The term hardware refers not only to the internal parts of the computer but also to its external parts, which are called peripheral devices.

FIGURE A-1: Computers are a part of daily life

● **What is a peripheral device?** A **peripheral device** is hardware that can be added to a computer system to expand what a computer can do. Popular peripheral devices include printers, media players, digital cameras, USB drives, scanners, and graphics tablets. Once your computer system is set up with its hardware and peripheral devices, it needs software in order to work as a computer.

● **What is software?** **Software** is a computer program that tells the computer how to perform tasks. You may have heard the terms word processing software, antivirus software, apps, or Web applications. These terms refer to some of the software that runs on your computer and other digital devices, such as your smartphone. There are many categories of software available for computers.

● **How do I use a computer?** To use a computer, you must input data or information. You use an **input device** (such as a keyboard, mouse, or touch screen) to input information. The input device and the computer work together to change the information into a series of electronic signals the computer can understand. Once the computer has the input, it processes the information and sends the processed information to an **output device**. Common output devices include monitors, printers, or speakers. As you work, you continue to input information and to use the output.

● **What is digitization, and why is it important in my daily life?** **Digitization** is the process of converting text, numbers, sound, photos, and video into data that can be processed by a computer. The advantage of digital images and sounds is that they can be easily stored, copied, and shared. Digital images have changed the photographic industry. Digital cameras have replaced film cameras. Digital imaging used in medical tests has had profound effects in the healthcare industry. Digital video is responsible for special effects in movies, new trends in 3D animation, portable video, and consumer interest in home video. Digital sound transformed the way music is marketed, sold, purchased, and played. Human speech can also be digitized. For example, when you call a business for help or information, digitized voice telephone systems understand and respond to your spoken words. GPS devices tell you the directions as your drive.

● **Is my smartphone a computer?** Yes, because a smartphone performs the four basic functions of a computer, it is considered a computer. For example, it accepts input—the phone numbers you type in. It processes the input, calling the number you entered. It stores data—keeping phone numbers in the address book. It outputs data—connects you to the phone you dial. When you think of a smartphone this way, it is a computer, but it is not a personal computer.

Other digital devices, such as mobile tablets, video game consoles, and media players, also perform the four basic functions of a computer. These devices accept input, process data, store data, and output information in the form of text, spoken words, music, video, and images. These digital devices share other computer characteristics, as well. For example, many tablet computers feature a small keyboard, others accept handwriting input, and some work with touch screen icons. Many digital devices today are the result of digital convergence.

● **What is digital convergence?** **Digital convergence** is the trend to blend several technologies that have distinct functions into a single product. An early example of digital convergence is the multipurpose machine that worked as a fax, printer, scanner, and telephone. Today many devices, such as mobile phones, portable media players, cameras, and GPSs, include features that overlap each other. These devices are evolving into a single device. Most mobile phones are smartphones. Figure A-2 shows an HP smartphone and the Apple iPhone. They include voice communication and other features such as text messaging, email, Web access, removable storage, camera, radio, digital music player, and software options for games, financial management, personal organizer, GPS, and maps.

FIGURE A-2: Smartphones

Storage inside unit

Keyboard
(for input)

Courtesy of Hewlett-Packard Company

Processor
inside unit
(for processing)

Speakers
(for output)

Touch screen
(for input and
for output)

© amriphoto/iStockphoto

Microphone
(for input)

How Computers Work

The parts of a computer system work together to accomplish these basic computer tasks—accept input, process data, store data, and produce output as information you can use. Most computers also are able to communicate to share information with other computers. Refer to Figure A-3 as you read more about how computers work.

Learning Objective 2:
Explain the four basic functions of a computer system

FIGURE A-3: Basic computer parts and functions

- Display device for output
- Speaker for sound output
- CD/DVD drive for storing and getting data
- System unit for processing and storing data
- Printer for producing output
- Camera for output and input
- Mouse for input
- Modem for communicating with other digital devices
- Keyboard for typing input
- Media for storing data

Hello!

Meet Polly

Top: Courtesy of MediaTechnics Corporation; © Sylvain Legare/Shutterstock.com; © Cengage Learning; Courtesy of MediaTechnics Corporation; bottom row: Courtesy of MediaTechnics Corporation; © Cengage Learning; © Tatiana Popova/Shutterstock.com; Courtesy of MediaTechnics Corporation; Courtesy of MediaTechnics Corporation

- **How do I turn on my computer?** A computer is often a computer system. You may need to press more than one switch or button to turn on the monitor, printer, speakers, and finally the computer. However, some computers, such as notebook or tablet computers, have one button or switch that turns on the entire computer system, including the computer, the monitor or display, and the speakers. Most computers take a few minutes to power up, and then you may be prompted to enter your **user ID** and **password**.

- **Why do I need a user ID and password?** You are assigned a user ID and password for security reasons. In a public setting, such as a school lab, you will usually be assigned a user ID and a password by the system administrator. If your personal computer asks for a user ID and password, you can create your own the first time you start the computer. You use that user ID and password every time you sign on to that computer and access the programs you have permission to use. Never share your user ID or password with anyone.

- **What does "run a program" mean?** It means to start a program. The instructions that tell a computer how to carry out the processing tasks are referred to as a **computer program**, or simply **program**. On mobile devices, such as tablets or smartphones, programs are called apps—short for applications. Once the program is running, it is ready for you to use.

- **How do I tell a computer what I want it to do?** You tell a computer what to do by interacting with it. You use a keyboard to type commands and other text. You use a mouse to access menus, as well as to click buttons and icons. On a computer with a touch screen, such as a tablet or smartphone, you touch and drag icons. Many digital devices today have on-screen keyboards. When you tell a computer what to do, you are providing input. Computer **input** is whatever is put into a computer system. Input can be supplied by a person, by the environment, or by another computer. Once information is input into a computer, it becomes data.

What do computers do with data? Computers process—that is, they work with—data in many ways. In the context of computing, data refers to the symbols that represent facts, objects, and ideas. In a computer, most **processing** takes place in a **processor** (also known as a **microprocessor**). The main processor in a computer is called the **central processing unit (CPU)**, which is sometimes described as the brain of the computer. A computer does two things with processed data. It stores the data and it outputs the data as information.

Is there a difference between computer memory and computer storage? Yes. **Memory** temporarily holds computer data waiting to be processed, stored, or output. **Storage** holds computer data on a permanent basis when it is not immediately needed for processing. While you are working on a document, it is in memory; it is not in storage until you save it for the first time. After you save the document as a computer file, it is stored on the hard drive or some other storage medium, such as a flash drive. It is also still in memory until you close the document, exit the program, or turn off the computer. You will learn more about storage and memory later in this book.

What are computer files? A computer file, or **file**, is a named collection of data that exists on a **storage medium**, such as a disk drive, CD, DVD, or flash drive. Every file has a **filename**, which should provide meaningful information about the file contents. The filename has two parts: the filename and the file extension. An example of a filename for a photo is Bridge.jpg. The name that you give the file is to the left of the period. The **file extension** is the period and two or more characters to the right of the period.

What is output and how do I use it? **Output** is the processed results produced by a computer. It is the information you want, such as reports, documents, music, graphs, and pictures. An output device (such as a monitor, a printer, or speakers) displays, prints, says, or otherwise transmits the results of processing.

Do all computers have network and Internet access? Many personal computer systems include built-in technology for wired or wireless connections to a computer network. Networking technology is useful for constructing a home network, connecting one or more computers to share devices, or connecting to public networks such as the Internet.

How do I turn off my computer? Usually, you turn off your computer by giving it a command, such as Shut Down. For a computer running Microsoft Windows, you click the on-screen Start button (see Figure A-4), and then click Shut Down. For an Apple computer, you click the Apple icon in the upper-left corner of the screen and then click Shut Down. For a tablet computer, such as an iPad, press and hold the Sleep/Wake button for a few seconds. When the red slider appears, slide the slider to turn off the device. After the computer powers down, you can manually turn off the printer and speakers, if necessary. Never turn off a computer by pressing the power switch, unless you are specifically instructed to do so.

FIGURE A-4: Shutting down a computer running Windows

Start button   Shut down button

Understanding the importance of stored programs

Modern computers use stored programs, that is, the instructions for a computing task are stored on the computer so they can be loaded quickly into a computer's memory when needed. These instructions can easily be replaced by different instructions when it is time for the computer to perform a different task. The stored program concept allows you to use your computer for one task, such as writing a letter, and then easily switch to a different computing task, such as editing a photo, looking at a Web page, or sending an email message.

Programs can be stored locally on your computer. An emerging trend is to use programs stored in the cloud. The **cloud** is mass storage on remote computers. **Cloud computing** refers to working in the cloud. You will learn more about the cloud and cloud computing later in this book.

Types of Computers

Computers are electronic devices that perform many tasks. Some types of computers are better for certain jobs than others. Computers are categorized according to how they are used, what they cost, their physical size, and their processing capability. Knowing about computer categories can help you buy the computer that best meets your needs.

Learning Objective 3:
Identify the main computer categories

● **Which type of computer is right for me?** You will most probably use a personal computer. A personal computer is designed to meet the computing needs of an individual for home, school, or small business use. It typically provides access to a wide variety of software, such as word processing, photo editing, budgeting and financial management, email, and Internet access. Personal computers include **desktop computers**, and **portable computers** such as **notebook computers** (sometimes called **laptop computers**), **netbooks**, and **tablet computers**.

● **If I get a desktop computer, will it fit on my desk**? Probably, yes. That is why it is called a desktop computer. A desktop computer's system unit can be housed in a vertical case or a horizontal case. Most horizontal cases are placed under the display device to save desk space. A vertical case can be placed on the desk, on the floor, or in a space beneath the desk. The case for a vertical system unit is often referred to as a tower. Tower units are the system unit of choice for computer owners who want to upgrade their system, such as by adding additional storage devices or a more powerful graphics card. It is easy to get inside a tower case and swap parts. Some manufacturers of desktop computers create an all-in-one unit. These computers build the computer technology into the back of a flat-panel screen or into a keyboard. See Figure A-5.

FIGURE A-5: Examples of personal desktop computers

Left: Courtesy of MediaTechnics Corporation; Right: Courtesy of Gateway; Used with permission from Microsoft

Tower computer   All-in-one desktop computer

● **What if I need to use my computer in different locations?** You will want to consider a portable computer. **Portable computers** include notebook computers, tablet computers, netbooks, and handheld computers. Examples of portable computers are shown in Figure A-6 and Figure A-7.

FIGURE A-6: Examples of portable personal computers

Top row, left: Courtesy of Hewlett-Packard Company; © Kathy Burns-Millyard/Shutterstock.com; Bottom row, left: PRNewsfoto/Radio Shack Corporation; Courtesy of MediaTechnics Corporation; Used with permission from Microsoft

Notebook   Convertible tablet

Netbook   Mobile tablet

● **What are the advantages of a notebook computer?** You might consider buying a notebook computer if you want to be able to move the computer from place to place, such as from home to school. Notebook computers have a clamshell design, which means they open and close on a hinge. When the computer is closed, the screen, pointing device, and keyboard are protected inside the case. Although notebook computers are much smaller than desktop computers, they are comparable when it comes to computing power. The two big differences between desktop and portable computers are their physical sizes and their cost.

- **Why should I consider a tablet computer?** A tablet computer is a portable computer that features a touch-sensitive screen. You can use this screen as a writing or a drawing pad. A tablet computer is similar in size to a notebook computer. The new mobile tablet computer is similar in size to a netbook computer. Most tablet computers can access the Internet or wireless networks. Most tablet computers are also configured to accept voice input. These capabilities are useful for people who use their computers while on the go.

- **What is a netbook?** A netbook computer offers more portability than a standard notebook computer. These small computers are scaled-down versions of standard clamshell-style notebook computers. They are typically only seven or eight inches wide and weigh about two pounds.

- **What if I just need a small portable computer that fits in my pocket?** Then, a **handheld computer** is just the answer. See Figure A-7. A handheld computer is one type of handheld digital device. There are a variety of handheld digital devices. These devices vary in how they can be used. Although these devices can be classified as computers, they are usually referred to by function, for example, as mobile phones, e-readers, or portable media players. The most popular handheld digital device is the smartphone.

FIGURE A-7: Handheld computer

Courtesy of Hewlett-Packard Company

Handheld digital devices usually have features such as removable storage, email, Web access, voice communications, built-in camera, and GPS. Handheld digital devices run computer programs, but, typically, they run special scaled-down versions of these programs. With its slow processing speed and small screen, a handheld computer is not powerful enough to handle many of the tasks that can be accomplished using desktop, notebook, tablet, or even netbook computers.

- **What are some other categories of computers I should know about?** There are three more general categories of computers you might hear people talk about.
  - **Workstations** are usually powerful desktop computers designed for specialized tasks that require a lot of processing speed, such as medical imaging, full-motion video graphics, and computer-aided design. Most are designed for creating and displaying three-dimensional and animated graphics.
  - A **mainframe computer** is a large and expensive computer capable of simultaneously processing data for hundreds or thousands of users. Mainframes are generally used by businesses, universities, or governments to provide centralized storage, processing, and management of large amounts of data where reliability, data security, and centralized control are necessary.
  - A computer is categorized as a **supercomputer** if, at the time it is built, it is one of the fastest computers in the world. Supercomputers can tackle tasks that would not be practical for other computers such as breaking codes and modeling worldwide weather systems.

- **What does it mean when I hear, "The server is down?" Is a server another type of computer?** The purpose of a **server** is to serve computers on a network (such as the Internet or a home network) by supplying them with data. Just about any personal computer, workstation, mainframe, or supercomputer can be configured to perform the work of a server. When you hear that a server is down, it means a computer connected to that server can't access the programs and files on that server.

Video game consoles

A videogame console, such as Nintendo's Wii, Nintendo's 3DS, Sony's PlayStation, or Microsoft's Xbox, is not generally referred to as a personal computer. Videogame consoles originated as simple digital devices that connected to a TV set and provided only a pair of joysticks for input. Today's videogame consoles contain processors that are equivalent to any processor found in a fast personal computer. They produce graphics, including 3D graphics, that rival those on sophisticated workstations. Many consoles include built-in Wi-Fi for easy connection to the Internet. Consoles can be used to watch movies, send and receive email, and participate in online activities such as multiplayer games. Despite these features, videogame consoles are not considered a replacement for a personal computer.

Personal Computers

The term **computer system** usually refers to a computer and all of the input, output, and storage devices that are connected to it. Despite cosmetic differences among personal computers (see Figure A-8), a personal computer system usually includes standard equipment or devices. These devices may vary in color, size, and design for different personal computers.

Learning Objective 4:
Describe digital devices that can be part of a personal computer

FIGURE A-8: Personal computer systems don't all look alike

From left: Courtesy of Gateway; © thesuperph/iStockphoto; © Cheng Xin/ iStockphoto; Courtesy of Fujitsu Technology Solutions; Used with permission from Microsoft

● **What are the basic parts of a desktop personal computer system?** Figure A-9 shows the basic parts of a typical desktop personal computer system. Refer to the figure as you read about each part.

■ **System unit**: The system unit is the case that holds the power supply, storage devices, and the circuit boards. It houses the main circuit board (also called the motherboard), which contains the processor.

■ **Display device**: Most computers have a **display device** called a **monitor**. The monitor is the primary output device. The monitor for a desktop computer is a separate part connected to the system unit. Output is displayed on the monitor screen.

■ **Keyboard**: Most computers are equipped with a **keyboard** as the primary input device. It is used to enter text and numbers.

■ **Mouse**: A **mouse** is a common input device designed to move and select on-screen graphical objects and controls.

■ **Storage devices**: A **storage device** is used to store data on a computer or to share data among computers. Storage devices are both input and output devices. Data is read from a storage medium and often can be written to a storage medium. Most personal computers

have more than one type of storage device. Each storage device uses a different storage medium. The primary storage device is the **hard drive** (also called **hard disk drive**). The hard drive is usually mounted inside the system unit.

Other storage devices can be used with a personal computer. A **USB flash drive** plugs directly into a USB port on the computer system unit. An external hard drive also plugs directly into a USB port. A CD drive, a DVD drive, a Blue-ray Disc (BD) drive, or a combination drive is usually mounted inside the system unit. These **optical drives** are storage devices that work with storage media such as CDs, DVDs, and BDs. They can be used to store computer data. Optical drives are also handy for playing audio CDs, DVD movies, and Blu-ray movies.

■ **Sound system**: A **sound system** is made up of speakers and a small circuit board called a **sound card**, required for high-quality music, narration, and sound effects. A desktop computer's sound card sends signals to external speakers. The sound card is an input and an output device, while speakers are output devices only.

■ **Printer**: A **printer** is an output device that produces computer-generated text, photographs, or graphic images on paper.

- **Web cam**: A **Web cam** allows you to capture video images using your computer. Software makes it possible to send and receive video in real time with another person to communicate with voice as well as images.
- **Peripheral devices**: There are many other peripheral devices that can be connected to a computer. For example, you can connect a portable **digital media player** and a **digital camera** in order to transfer music and photos between the devices and the computer system.

● **Does a portable computer have all these parts?** Yes, but a portable computer, such as a notebook computer, is a single unit that includes the system unit, a built-in flat-panel monitor, a built-in keyboard, and built-in speakers. Many new portable computers include a built-in Web cam. Other devices, such as a printer, can be connected to a portable computer in the same way they can be connected to a desktop computer. Portable computers can also be part of a network and can have Internet access.

● **How do I know if my computer has network and Internet access?** Many personal computer systems include built-in technology for wired or wireless connections to a computer network. Networking is useful for connecting to a home network or to public networks, such as the Internet. Internet connections require a **modem**. Modems can be built into portable computers. For tablets you can use an aircard or portable modem, which works like a mobile phone. For Internet access using a smartphone, the modem is built into the device. Modems for cable, satellite, and other types of Internet access from your home or office are usually separate devices.

● **What is a computer network?** A **computer network** consists of two or more computers and other devices that are connected for the purpose of sharing data and programs. For example, a **LAN (local area network)** is simply a computer network that is located within a limited geographical area, such as your home, a school computer lab, or a small business. If your computer is on a network, you can easily access files on other computers that are on the same network.

● **What parts of a computer system do I absolutely need?** You need a system unit for processing and storage, a monitor for output, and a keyboard and pointing device for input. Many people also want a printer and a portable storage device, such as a flash drive.

FIGURE A-9: Typical desktop computer system with examples of peripherals

Screen Monitor Speaker System unit CD drive DVD drive Hard drive (inside system unit) Speaker (sound card inside system unit) Printer Mouse Keyboard Web cam Digital camera Digital media player Cable modem and wireless router USB flash drive Card reader

Top: Courtesy of MediaTechnics Corporation; © Natalila Silverina/Shutterstock.com; Used with permission from Microsoft; Courtesy of MediaTechnics Corporation; Bottom row: Courtesy of MediaTechnics Corporation; Courtesy of MediaTechnics Corporation; © Norman Chan/Shutterstock.com; © Tatiana Popova/Shutterstock.com; Courtesy of MediaTechnics Corporation; Used with permission from Microsoft

Computer Software

A computer needs software to work. Software provides the instructions that tell a computer how to perform tasks. There are two main categories of software: operating system software and application software. Every computer has an operating system. But, as a computer user, you are probably most familiar with application software. You use application software to look at Web pages on the Internet, write reports, create budgets, view and edit photographs, play games, as well as other tasks you do using your computer. The operating system you have on your computer determines the software you can run on your computer.

Learning Objective 5:
Define software and give examples of operating systems

● **What is an operating system?** An **operating system (OS)** is the master controller for all the activities that take place within a computer system. An operating system is classified as **system software**. Its primary purpose is to help the computer system monitor itself in order to function efficiently. Most people have only one operating system running on their computer and most personal computers can run only one operating system at one time. There are several different operating systems available for personal computers, such as Windows, Mac OS, and Linux. The two most popular operating systems for personal computers are Windows and Mac OS. While these two operating systems look and even work in a similar way, they are different. Each is designed to run on different computer platforms.

● **What is a computer platform?** A **computer platform** determines the hardware and software of the computer system. Two of the most important factors that define a computer's platform are the processor and the OS. The Windows operating system was designed specifically for PCs. The PC platform is sometimes called the Windows platform. The Macintosh OS was designed specifically for Macintosh computers, which are based on a proprietary design and manufactured almost exclusively by Apple Computer, Inc. The Linux OS is usually used as an alternative to the Windows OS.

Today, many Mac computers use the same processors as PCs. If you have a Mac computer with an Intel processor (sometimes called an Intel Mac), you can install the Windows OS on that machine and run Windows software.

● **What is Windows software?** Windows software is software designed to run on a PC platform. Generally, software designed to run on a PC platform will not run on a Mac platform, and software designed to run on a Mac platform will not run on a PC platform. When shopping for new software, it is important to read the package to make sure that the software is designed to work with your computer platform.

● **How do I use the operating system?** Most of the time, you use the operating system without realizing it. See Figure A-10. You interact with the operating system for certain tasks, such as starting programs and finding data files. How you use the operating system depends on the user interface associated with the operating system. Operating systems use a **graphical user interface (GUI)**.

FIGURE A-10: The operating system makes it possible to interact with the computer

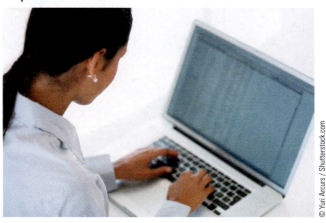

© Yuri Arcurs / Shutterstock.com

PCs and Macs

People generally refer to personal computers either as PCs, which run a version of Windows software, or as Macs, which run Macintosh software. PCs are manufactured and distributed by a variety of vendors. Macs are almost exclusively developed and distributed by Apple Computer Company.

FIGURE A-11: Popular elements of a GUI

Icon

Thumbnail

Taskbar

Application buttons

Gadget

Open windows

Desktop

Scroll bar

Used with permission from Microsoft

Notification area with icons

Show desktop button

See Figure A-11. A GUI displays on-screen icons, menus, buttons, and other graphical controls. These controls are manipulated by a mouse or other pointing device. For example, you might click an icon to start an application program, or drag time slots on a calendar to create appointments. If you are using a touch screen, you touch, tap, and drag icons with your fingers.

● **Does my mobile phone use the same OS as my personal computer?** No, mobile devices use an OS designed specifically for mobile devices, such as Android (see Figure A-12), BlackBerry OS, iOS for

FIGURE A-12: Operating system for mobile devices

Courtesy of Motorola Solutions

iPhones, or a mobile version of an existing OS, such as Windows Phone. Mobile OSs are also known as mobile software platforms or handheld operating systems.

● **How does the operating system help me do my work?** The operating system runs the software on your computer. **Application software** is a general term used to classify the programs that help you use the computer to carry out tasks. Word processing software, for example, helps you create, edit, and print documents. Browser software helps you view Web pages on the Internet. Each application software program has its own name, such as Microsoft Word or Internet Explorer. Your computer can run more than one application program at one time.

● **What are apps? Apps**, sometimes called **mobile apps**, are software programs designed to run on mobile devices, such as your smartphone. Apps are available for download from a variety of online stores. They are usually available for free or a small fee.

● **If my computer runs Windows and my friend's computer runs Mac OS X, can we share our files?** Sharing files depends on system compatibility. Some application software has been created so one version exists for the Windows platform and another for the Macintosh platform. You are able to share your files with your friend, as long as your friend has the same software installed on his or her computer.

The Internet and the Web

You can use the Internet to look for information. You can use the Internet to shop. You can use the Internet to share photos and videos. You can use it to communicate with friends, coworkers, or family. You can even use the Internet to buy products and services, look for a job, or plan a trip. The Internet offers abundant resources. This lesson will help you understand how you can use the Internet and the Web in your daily life.

Learning Objective 6:
Define the Internet and explain how to navigate Web pages

● **What is the Internet?** The **Internet** is the largest computer network in the world. It is a collection of local, regional, national, and international computer networks. These networks are linked together to exchange data and share processing tasks.

● **How do I access the Internet?** To access the Internet your computer must have special hardware and software. You need equipment called a router. The **router** connects to your computer and to the Internet. Computers connect to the Internet either with wires or wirelessly. To connect to the Internet you also need an **Internet Service Provider**. This is a company that provides the service of connecting the router to the Internet, usually for a monthly fee.

● **Is the Web the same as the Internet?** The **Web** (short for **World Wide Web**) is a collection of **Web pages** that are interconnected through the use of **hypertext** or links. The Internet is the network that carries Web pages to computers. Web pages can include text, photos, videos, animations, and sounds. The Web is the part of the Internet you will probably use most often.

● **Why would I use the Internet?** You might use the Internet to research, and then buy products and services. For example, you can buy airline tickets through the Internet. If you want to sell a product or service, you can use the Internet to help you run your own small business. See Figure A-13. You might use the Internet to share photographs with family and friends. At a job, you can use the Internet to work on documents with coworkers. Most banks have Web sites their customers use for bill paying and online banking. You might use the Internet to communicate with others.

FIGURE A-13: Using the Web to help run a business

Image courtesy of Photography by Toine

● **How do I view a Web page?** To view Web pages on your computer, you need a software program called a Web browser. Popular **Web browsers** include Microsoft Internet Explorer, Google Chrome, Mozilla FireFox, and Apple Safari. You enter a URL in the Address box of the browser window. If you are viewing a Web page, you can also click a link to view another Web page.

● **What is a link?** A **link** (also called a hyperlink) is text, a graphic, or other object on a Web page that is "linked" to another Web page or another area on the current Web page. You click a link to "jump" to another Web page, Web site, or place on the same Web page. Links are the main tool you will use to navigate among Web pages.

● **What is a URL?** Every Web page has a unique address called a **URL (Uniform Resource Locator)**. The URL for a Web page indicates the computer on which it is stored, its location on the Web server, the folder name or names indicating where it is stored, its filename, and its file extension. Most browsers provide a space near the top of the window for entering URLs. Figure A-14 identifies the parts of the URL for a

National Park Service Web page. A URL never contains a space, even after a punctuation mark. An underline character is sometimes used to give the appearance of a space between words.

FIGURE A-14: Parts of a URL

http://www.nps.gov/yose/index.htm

| Web protocol standard | Web server name | Folder name | Document name and file extension |

© Cengage Learning

● **What does it mean if I see http:// in the Address box?** Most URLs begin with http://. **HTTP (Hypertext Transfer Protocol)** is the technology used to transport Web pages over the Internet. You might also see https://, which is used for additional security at Web sites such as those that offer banking and shopping. When typing a URL, you do not have to type the http://. Typing www.cengage.com/coursetechnology/ works just as well as typing http://www.cengage.com/coursetechnology/. Be sure to use the correct type of slash—always a forward slash (/).

● **How do I navigate a Web site?** Web pages on a related topic are often grouped together to create a

Web site. Most Web sites have a main page, the **home page**, which acts as a doorway to the rest of the Web site pages. Usually, the Web pages have a navigation bar that contains links you click to move to other pages in the Web site. See Figure A-15. In addition, your browser has buttons to help you navigate the Web. For example, the browser's Back button lets you retrace your steps to view pages that you've seen previously.

● **How do I find information on the Web?** The term **search site** refers to a Web site that provides a variety of tools to help you find information on the Web. A **keyword** is any word or phrase that you type to describe the information that you are trying to find. Based on the keyword you input, the search site uses its **search engine** to provide a list of possible Web sites that may have the information you are looking for. The list is actually links (also called hits) to Web pages. So you can click each link to see if any Web site in the list has what you are looking for. You should try different variations on your keyword to improve your results. Also, search sites have different ways of ranking the search results. As a result, if you use two different search sites to search for the same keyword, you will probably get different results.

FIGURE A-15: Navigating a Web page

Click a link to view a different page

Type a search word or phrase, then click Go

Click the arrow to see a list, then click a national park name

www.nps.gov

Web apps and working in the cloud

A **Web application (Web app)** is software that you access through a Web browser. Instead of running on your computer, much of the program for the software runs on a distant computer, often called the **cloud**, connected to the Internet or other network. Web apps are available for many tasks, such as email, calendars, photo sharing, games, and even word processing. Web apps allow you to work on projects with people in multiple locations. Working with a Web app allows you to store your work in the cloud. When you use cloud storage, you can access your files from any computer that has a browser and Internet access.

Mobile Web apps are designed to work on mobile devices. Mobile Web apps have features designed for portability and a small screen.

The cloud has some risks. A security breach of a cloud provider could expose the data of all its users. Outages at the cloud provider, on the Internet in general, or locally at your computer can mean that you cannot get to your programs and files. If a cloud provider goes out of business without notice (and there are no regulations to prevent this from happening), all your data could become unavailable.

How to Communicate Using Digital Devices

Each year, countless email messages are sent around the world over the Internet. Millions of messages cross paths as instant messages. Even more text messages flow between smartphones. Social networks are buzzing with posts. This lesson will help you understand the many ways you can communicate digitally with family and friends.

> ### Learning Objective 7:
> Explain ways to use the Internet and digital devices to communicate with others

- **What is email?** **Email** (short for **electronic mail**) is a message sent electronically over the Internet. To send an email message, you must have an email account.

- **How do I get an email account?** You get an **email account** through an email provider. There are many providers, such as your Internet service provider, university, Gmail (through Google), or Hotmail (through Microsoft Windows Live). Your email account includes a storage area, often called a **mailbox**. Depending on who provides your email account, you will either be assigned an **email address** or you will create one. Figure A-16 shows the parts of an email address.

FIGURE A-16: Parts of an email address

David_velez@rutgers.edu		
User ID	"at" symbol	Name of email provider

© Cengage Learning

- **Do I need a special computer to send and receive email?** No, but your computer or smartphone must be able to connect to the Internet and it must have email software installed. Email software usually includes an address book to help you maintain contact information, including email addresses of people you contact frequently.

- **What does an email message look like?** An **email message** has several parts. Every email message includes the recipient's email address, the address of anyone who is receiving a copy of the message, the message subject, the body, and the name of any file attachments. The body of the email contains your message. An email message is created in a form, which often includes buttons for formatting text, attaching files, or adding additional recipients as courtesy (Cc), or blind courtesy (Bcc) copies. Basic email activities include writing, reading, replying to, and forwarding messages.

- **Do I need to be at my computer when my friend sends me the email?** No. Email is based on store-and-forward technology. Emails that cannot be sent directly to their destinations are temporarily stored until they are forwarded to the email mailbox.

- **Can I send a file or picture through email?** Yes. In addition to the body text of an email message, you can send documents, spreadsheets, digital photos, video, and sounds. Any file that travels with an email message is called an **email attachment**.

- **Can I use the Internet to have real-time conversations with people?** Yes. One popular way you can do this is participating in a **chat group**, which consists of several people who connect to the Internet and communicate in real time by typing notes to each other. A private version of chat is called **instant messaging (IM)**. IM allows you to send text messages, images, and hyperlinks back and forth to another person instantly. If you are online at the same time as the person you want to chat or instant message, you can type messages back and forth in real time. There is no limit on the number of characters in your chat or IM.

   You can also use the Internet to talk to people in real-time thanks to **Internet telephony**, also called **Voice Over IP (VoIP)**. VoIP allows voice conversations to travel over the Internet. VoIP requires special software at both ends of the conversation. Instead of using a telephone, you have to use a headset with a microphone connected to a computer. VoIP providers, such as Skype, also offer video conversations. If you and the person you are talking with both have a Web cam connected to your computers, you can see each other while you are talking. Other popular ways of communicating are through forums, wikis, blogs, and social networking.

● **What are forums, wikis, and blogs?** An **Internet forum** is a Web site where you can post comments to discussion threads. Threads are simply topics. Comments can be read at any time by others who visit the forum. Most forums have a moderator who monitors the discussions, weeds out troublesome participants, and handles membership requests.

A **wiki** is a collaborative Web site that allows people to add to and modify material posted by others. Participants can post content on a topic, and others can change it. Wikis can also include discussion pages where people just comment on topic material. The best known is Wikipedia.

The term **blog** is derived from the phrase Web log. It refers to a personal journal focusing on a single topic or a variety of topics. The information in a blog is usually available to the public. Some blog sites allow you to restrict access to those you invite to read your blog. People often create blogs to share travel adventures, political views, or important events in their lives.

● **What is social networking?** **Social networking** is an online networking activity that allows registered members to communicate with others in the network. You can use online social networks, such as Google+, LinkedIn, MySpace, and Facebook. Twitter, another social networking option, uses 140 character messages for blogging. If you have a Twitter account, you can post or follow posted messages that can lead to more extensive information. See Figure A-17.

To become a member of an online social network, you fill out a questionnaire to create your profile and to identify a list of friends. You can then interact with your friends or with friends of friends who are members of the same social network. This networking technique offers a level of security because members are interacting with friends or with friends of friends, rather than with strangers. Social networking sites provide private messaging options.

Social networking sites all have mobile apps to make it easy to follow and network from smartphones. In addition to using your mobile phone to social network, you can use it to send text messages.

● **What are text messages?** **Text messages** are typed messages you send using your smartphone, or mobile device. Depending on the service, text messages can be 140 to 160 characters or less. You can send text messages by using the Web sites of mobile providers but it is more common to use your mobile device to send text messages. If your mobile phone service has Multimedia Messaging Service (MMS), you can send pictures and video in addition to text. You do not need the added features of a smartphone to send text messages from a mobile phone.

The line between when to use your computer and when to use your smartphone to communicate is blurring. Computers and smartphones are allowing you to communicate in new and exciting ways with your circle of family, friends, and coworkers. See Figure A-18.

FIGURE A-18: Social networking with friends, family, and coworkers

© Luba V Nel/Shutterstock.com

FIGURE A-17: You can use Twitter for social networking

© 2011 Twitter

How to Protect Your Privacy, Data, and Devices

Whether you are surfing in the ocean or surfing on the Web. Whether you are buying an item in the mall or clicking to purchase airline tickets online, security and safety should always be the primary concern. Computers and digital communication have built-in dangers. You have to safeguard your health, safety, and personal data. You also need to take care of your digital devices so they work properly when you need them. This lesson will help you avoid potential pitfalls in the digital world so you can enjoy safe computing.

Learning Objective 8:
Explain how to protect your digital data and devices

● **What can go wrong?** Many things can happen. Someone might steal your computer, or you might misplace it. Your data might get damaged or stolen. A thief might steal your credit card numbers or, worse, your identity. You might drop your computer or spill coffee on it. See Figure A-19. The list of what can go wrong goes on and on. Fortunately, there are simple steps you can take to prevent things from going wrong.

FIGURE A-19: Be careful with your computer

©Mikael Damkier/Shutterstock.com

● **How can I prevent things from going wrong?** You can use common sense and tools to protect yourself, your data, and your digital devices. To protect yourself, you must safeguard your personal data. To protect your data, you must install an antivirus program, a firewall, and other programs that help keep your data safe. To protect your digital devices, you must treat them with care.

● **What is at risk if my computer is stolen?** Your identity is the biggest risk factor if your computer is stolen. Why? Because your computer contains data about you, such as your bank account information and credit card numbers, and PINs. A thief can use stolen data to assume your identity, empty your checking and savings accounts, run up debts, get into legal difficulties, ruin your credit rating, and cause you no end of trouble.

● **How can I keep my computer from being stolen?** You should never leave your computer unattended in a public place. You should never leave your computer visible in a car, even in a locked car. If you live in a group situation, such as a dormitory, anchor your computer to your desk with a specially designed lock you can buy at most electronics stores.

In addition to these precautions, be sure to password-protect your computer. Then, if a thief steals your computer, he or she will need the password to access your data. Until the password is entered, your data is off limits. So, even if a thief is able to turn on the computer, he or she will not be able to get at the information on your computer.

● **What should I use for a password?** Use a **password** you can remember but that others cannot guess. Here are some tips for creating a unique password.

■ Use at least eight characters, mixing numbers with letters, as in m3p1e8.

■ Do not use your name, birthday, the name of a family member, or your pet's name.

■ Do not use a word that can be found in the dictionary.

■ Do not keep a written copy of your password near your computer.

While passwords keep your data safe from unwanted visitors, they do not keep your data safe from malware.

● **What is malware?** **Malware**, also known as **malicious software**, is a type of software that can do harm to your computer data. There are different types of malware, such as viruses, worms, Trojan horses, and spyware. On a personal level, malware can steal data or destroy files. On a larger scale, malware can create network traffic jams that affect Web sites or corporate computer systems. Malware is often installed on your computer without your knowledge. For example, malware can be installed behind the scenes while you download software. See Figure A-20. Malware is created by **hackers**, people that want to steal or damage your data or assume your identity.

FIGURE A-20: Know that your downloads are safe

© iConcept/Shutterstock.com

● **How can I protect my computer from malware?**
You should install programs, such as an antivirus program, a firewall, or a malware detection program, that can stop malware from being installed. These programs can also find and delete any malware that slipped through the safety net and got installed. You can use these programs to scan files to be sure they are safe to download. These programs can keep your computer malware free and your data safe. You will learn more about malware later in this book.

Not only computers but all digital devices, including smartphones, can get malware. It is important to find and install programs to protect your device from malware. It is also important to keep the anti-malware software on all your digital devices up to date.

● **Do I need to protect my privacy when using digital communication?** Yes. When you are social networking, posting to Web pages, chatting, IMing, sending email messages, or communicating in any way over the Internet, you have to protect your personal information. Table A-1 provides some guidelines to help you protect your personal information and your privacy.

● **How can I limit who sees my digital communications?** Anything you write, or any photo you upload can be copied, posted, or forwarded around the Internet with just a few clicks. Anyone can read or see your digital communications unless you take some precautions. Here are some tips on how to limit who has access to your electronic messages.
When emailing…
- Click Reply to reply only to the person who sent an email message. Clicking Reply limits who sees your response. Click Reply All if you want your response sent to everyone who received the original email message (except the Bcc recipients).
- Use the Cc: feature to include people you want to read your email but that you don't want to respond to the message.
- Use the Bcc: feature to blind copy your email to people without revealing to the Send to and Cc: recipients who else got the message.
- Create a group if you have people you send messages to regularly. This will ensure all the people in the group get the same message. It will also save time because you only have to enter the group name and not type the email of each person in the group.
When posting…
- Check the options to identify those people or groups you want to see a message you post on a blog or wall of a social networking site. Some sites post to the general public if you don't specify otherwise.
- Be sure you have permission from anyone in a picture when you post or tag the photo; only post your own photos and graphics.
- Regard wall messages, posted photos, and chat messages as postcards that can be read and seen by anyone. Do not say or share anything you would not want repeated or broadcast to the world!

TABLE A-1: Ways to protect your privacy

Tips	Tips
Do not publish or post personal information, such as your home address, passwords, Social Security number, phone number, or account numbers.	Do not submit data to a social networking site until you've read its privacy policy and have made sure that you can remove your data when you no longer want to participate.
If asked for personal information, verify the Web site is legitimate, or make a phone call to confirm that you have to submit the information, and then confirm that the information will be securely transmitted and stored.	Avoid financial transactions when using a public computer. Never click the save my password box and make sure you log out from password-protected sites.
Be wary of contacts you make in public chat rooms and on social networking sites.	Never use a password-protected Web site on a public computer that doesn't give you the option to save the password.

© Cengage Learning

Talking Points: Who Is Reading Your Email?

When you drop an envelope into the corner mailbox, you probably expect it to arrive at its destination unopened, with its contents kept safe from prying eyes. When you make a phone call, you might assume that your conversation will proceed unmonitored by wiretaps or other listening devices. When you send an email, can you be sure it will be read only by the person to whom it is addressed?

In the United States, the Electronic Communications Privacy Act of 2000 prohibits the use of intercepted email as evidence unless a judge approves a search warrant. But, that does not mean the government is not reading your email. Heightened security concerns after the September 11, 2001 terrorist attacks resulted in the rapid passage of the Patriot Act, which became law on October 26, 2001. In an effort to assist law enforcement officials, the Patriot Act relaxes the rules for obtaining and implementing search warrants and lowers the Fourth Amendment standard for obtaining a court order to require an email provider to produce email logs and addresses.

> **Think of your email as a postcard, rather than a letter, and save your controversial comments for face-to-face or telephone conversations.**

To eavesdrop on email from suspected terrorists and other criminals, the FBI developed a technology that scans through email messages entering and leaving an email provider's email system to find email associated with a person who is under investigation. Privacy advocates are concerned because this software scans all messages that pass through an email provider, not just those messages sent from or received by a particular individual.

Although law enforcement agencies are required to obtain a court order before intercepting email, no such restriction exists for employers who want to monitor employee email. It is a known fact that many U.S. businesses monitor employee email; however, intentional eavesdropping is only one way in which the contents of your email messages might become public. For example, the recipient of your email can forward it to one or more persons—people you never intended it to reach. Your email messages could pop up on a technician's screen in the course of system maintenance, updates, or repairs. Also, keep in mind that email messages—including those you delete from your own computer—can be stored on backups of your email provider's email server. You also need to be aware that some email providers retain your email and gather information about you in exchange for the email service they provide.

You need to know what information your email provider collects via your email and what the email provider does with that collected information. For example, some Web-based email providers—particularly those that make you look at ads in exchange for free accounts—collect information on how often you log in and they monitor your keystrokes to find out which links you click. Email providers claim they gather this information to use internally so they can deliver the best possible service, prevent fraud, and select the ads for products that you are most likely to buy. Before selecting an email provider, find out what information the email provider collects, and then you can decide if that is acceptable to you.

You might wonder if such open access to your email and your ad-viewing habits is legal. The answer in most cases is yes. The United States Omnibus Crime Control and Safe Streets Act of 1968 and the Electronic Communications Privacy Act of 1986 prohibit public and private employers from engaging in surreptitious surveillance of employee activity through the use of electronic devices. However, two exceptions to these privacy statutes exist. The first exception permits an employer to monitor email if one party to the communication consents to the monitoring. An employer must inform employees of this policy before undertaking any monitoring. The second exception permits employers to monitor employees' email if a legitimate business need exists and the monitoring takes place within the business-owned email system.

Employees generally have not been successful in defending their rights to email privacy because courts have ruled that an employee's right to privacy does not outweigh a company's rights and interests. Courts seem to agree that because a company owns and maintains its email system, it has the right to monitor the email messages the system carries.

Like employees of a business, students who use a school's email system cannot be assured of email privacy. When a CalTech student was accused of sexually harassing a female student by sending lewd email to her and her boyfriend, investigators retrieved all of the student's email from the archives of the email server. The student was expelled from the university even though he claimed that the email had been spoofed to make it look as though he had sent it, when it had actually been sent by someone else.

Why would an employer want to know the contents of employee email? Why would a school be concerned with the correspondence of its students? It is probably true that some organizations simply snoop on the off chance that important information might be discovered. Other organizations have more legitimate reasons for monitoring email. An organization that owns an email system can be held responsible for the consequences of actions related to the contents of email messages on that system. For example, a school has a responsibility to protect students from harassment. If it fails to do so, it can be sued along with the author of the offending email message. Organizations also recognize a need to protect themselves from false rumors and industrial espionage. For example, a business wants to know if an employee is supplying its competitor with information on product research and development.

Many schools and businesses have established email privacy policies that explain the conditions under which students or employees can and cannot expect their emails to remain private. These policies are sometimes displayed when the computer boots or a new user logs in. Court decisions, however, seem to support the notion that because an organization owns and operates an email system, the email messages on that system are also the property of the organization. The individual who authors an email message

does not own all rights related to it. The company, school, or organization that supplies an email account can, therefore, legally monitor the messages sent and received via that account. You should use your email account with the expectation that some of your email will be read from time to time. Think of your email as a postcard, rather than a letter, and save your controversial comments for face-to-face or telephone conversations.

> "An organization that owns an email system can be held responsible for the consequences of actions related to the contents of email messages on that system."

Expand the Ideas

1. Do you believe that your email will probably be read only by your intended recipient? Knowing that your email is not private, will you be more careful in what you send via the email system? Why or why not?

2. Should the laws be changed to make it illegal for employers to monitor email without court approval? Why or why not?

3. Should the privacy laws governing an email account at your place of work differ from an account you purchase from an email service provider? Why or why not?

What is spam?

Spam is unwanted electronic junk mail that arrives in your email Inbox. A majority of today's proliferation of spam is generated by marketing firms that harvest email addresses from mailing lists, membership applications, and Web sites. Some spam messages advertise illegal products. Others are outright scams to try to get you to download a virus, divulge your bank account numbers, or send in money for products you will never receive. Beware of offers that seem just too good to be true—these offers are probably spam.

A **spam filter** automatically routes advertisements and other junk mail to either the Deleted Items or a spam folder maintained by your email provider. Spam filters can be effective for blocking spam and other unwanted emails, however, they sometimes block email messages you want. Be sure to examine your Deleted Items folder periodically to make sure the spam filters are not blocking emails that you want. If emails you want are in your Deleted Items or spam folder, reset your filters.

Key Terms & Unit Review

Key Terms

App
Application software
Blog
Browser
Central processing unit (CPU)
Chat group
Cloud
Cloud computing
Computer
Computer network
Computer platform
Computer program
Computer system
Desktop computer
Digital camera
Digital convergence
Digital media player
Digital revolution
Digital technology
Digitization
Display device
Email (electronic mail)
Email account
Email address
Email attachment
Email message

File
File extension
Filename
Graphical User Interface (GUI)
Hacker
Handheld computer
Hard disk drive
Hard drive
Hardware
Home page
HTTP (Hypertext Transfer Protocol)
Hypertext
Input
Input device
Instant messaging (IM)
Internet
Internet forum
Internet service provider (ISP)
Internet telephony
Keyboard
Keyword
LAN (local area network)
Laptop computer
Link

Mailbox
Mainframe computer
Malicious software
Malware
Memory
Microprocessor
Mobile app
Modem
Monitor
Mouse
Netbook
Notebook computer
Operating system
Optical drive
Output
Output device
Password
Peripheral device
Personal computer (PC)
Portable computer
Printer
Processing
Processor
Program
Router
Search engine
Search site

Server
Social networking
Software
Sound card
Sound system
Spam
Spam filter
Storage
Storage device
Storage medium
Supercomputer
System software
System unit
Tablet computer
Text messaging
URL (Uniform Resource Locator)
USB flash drive
User ID
Voice Over IP (VoIP)
Web (World Wide Web)
Web browser
Web cam
Web page
Web site
Wiki
Workstation

Unit Review

1. Make sure that you can define each of the key terms in this unit in your own words. Select 10 of the terms with which you are unfamiliar and write a sentence for each of them.

2. Explain how you use computers in your daily life.

3. Explain the basic functions of a computer: input, processing, storing, and output.

4. Identify and describe the purpose of each of the components of a basic personal computer system.

5. Describe the difference between an operating system and application software.

6. Explain why the stored program concept is important to computers.

7. List at least three activities that are not communications related and that you can accomplish using the Internet. If you have used the Internet, write a brief paragraph explaining how you benefitted from using it.

8. Make a list of at least three different ways you can use the Internet to communicate with other people.

9. Name the parts of a URL.

10. List the advantages and disadvantages of at least three types of computers as described in this unit and why you might choose one over the other.

Concepts Review

Select the best answer.

1. Which of the following is not a type of personal computer?
   - a. mainframe
   - b. notebook
   - c. desktop
   - d. netbook

2. The part that is considered the brains of the computer is called the _____ processing unit.
   - a. main
   - b. central
   - c. operating
   - d. local

3. The idea of stored programs means that instructions for a computing task can be loaded into a computer's _____.
   - a. hard drive
   - b. software
   - c. operating system
   - d. memory

4. The system _____ houses important parts such as the circuit boards, processor, power supply, and storage devices.
   - a. processor
   - b. memory
   - c. drive
   - d. unit

5. A device that expands a computer's capability is called a(n) _____ device.
   - a. input
   - b. peripheral
   - c. output
   - d. processing

6. A(n) _____ is a computer device that makes it possible to capture video.
   - a. netbook
   - b. scanner
   - c. mp3 player
   - d. Web cam

7. A(n) _____ system is the software that acts as the master controller for all of the activities that take place within a computer system.
   - a. application
   - b. processor
   - c. digital
   - d. operating

8. A computer _____ consists of two or more computers and other devices that are connected for the purpose of sharing data and programs.
   - a. system
   - b. network
   - c. netbook
   - d. hardware

9. Android is a type of _____.
   - a. power supply
   - b. operating system
   - c. blog
   - d. network

10. A _____ is the system unit of choice for computer owners who want to upgrade because it is easy to get inside and swap parts.
    - a. tower unit
    - b. notebook
    - c. netbook
    - d. PDA

11. The _____ often provides a clue to the contents of a file.
    - a. browser
    - b. application
    - c. filename
    - d. operating system

12. A _____ computer uses a touch screen keyboard for typing.
    - a. desktop unit
    - b. notebook
    - c. tower unit
    - d. tablet

13. A(n) _____ is a personal journal posted on the Web for access by the public.
    - a. chat
    - b. email
    - c. instant message
    - d. blog

14. An email account has a unique address that typically consists of a user ID, the _____ symbol, and the name of the computer that maintains the mailbox.
    - a. X
    - b. *
    - c. @
    - d. #

15. Every Web page has a unique address called a(n) _____.
    - a. ARL
    - b. URL
    - c. RUL
    - d. LUR

16. Facebook and LinkedIn are examples of Web sites that provide social _____.
    - a. chatting
    - b. blogging
    - c. networking
    - d. email

17. To find information on the Web, it is best to use a _____ engine.
    - a. Web
    - b. home
    - c. search
    - d. program

18. A Web _____ is a series of Web pages on a specific topic.
    - a. blog
    - b. group
    - c. site
    - d. URL

19. Digital _____ is the trend in which several technologies with distinct functionalities evolve to form a single product.
    - a. revolution
    - b. electronics
    - c. divide
    - d. convergence

20. A(n) _____ is any word or phrase that you type in a search engine to describe the information that you are trying to find.
    - a. keyword
    - b. adjective
    - c. verb
    - d. Wiki

Independent Challenges

Independent Challenge 1

When discussing computers and computer concepts, it is important to use proper terminology. Unit A presented many computer terms that describe computer equipment. If you would like to explore any of the terms in more detail, there are online dictionaries that can help you expand your understanding of these terms. You can even use Webopedia to help you better learn about specific computer terms, for example, a tablet computer. See Figure A-21.

FIGURE A-21: Webopedia Web site

Provided by Webopedia.com

For this Independent Challenge:

1. Write a one-page paper that describes the computer you use most frequently.

2. Refer to the key terms used in this unit and use terms from this unit to describe the parts of your computer, including their functions.

3. Underline each key term that you used in your paper.

4. Follow your instructor's directions for submitting your paper either as an email attachment or as a printed document.

Independent Challenge 2

In 1982, the computer gained recognition in *TIME* magazine when it was named "Machine of the Year." That year, fewer than 10% of U.S. households had a computer. Maybe that is because working on a stand-alone computer wasn't for everyone. When computers first became available, people weren't tempted to spend the money to buy a computer and enter the digital revolution unless they were interested in typing up corporate reports or school papers, crunching numbers for accounting purposes, or playing computer games. But as interest in computers and in the Internet gained popularity, social scientists worried that people would become increasingly isolated as they focused on computer activities rather than social ones.

In 2010, Time magazine named Mark Zuckerberg the Person of the Year. He is the founder of Facebook, the social networking Web site that has arguably changed the way people throughout the world interact socially through computers. As of July 2010, Facebook had reached 500 million members—the equivalent of connecting with eight percent of the world's population.

Imagine that the producers for a television game show ask you to help them write computer-related questions for the next show. They want to know the impact of social networking. They want to find out how computer literate people have become. To help the producers, you will compose a set of 10 questions based on the information provided in Unit A. Each question should be in multiple-choice format with four possible answers.

For this Independent Challenge:

1. Write 10 questions that test a person's knowledge of the concepts covered in Unit A: two very simple questions, five questions of medium difficulty, and three difficult questions. Each question should be on an index card.

2. For each question, indicate the correct answer on the back of each card and the page in this book on which the answer can be found.

3. Gather in small groups and take turns asking each other the questions.

Independent Challenge 3

As a busy student, you are constantly on the go. When you are away from your home, you still need access to the Internet, your calendar, and contacts. For this independent challenge, assume that you have a basic mobile phone. You are considering upgrading your mobile phone to a smartphone. You are unsure if it makes sense to get a new smartphone or to invest in a tablet computer and keep your current mobile phone. You have heard about great apps for smartphones as well as tablet computers. It is time for you to start researching your options.

You can buy your digital device from a brick-and-mortar store (such as Best Buy), from an online communications company (such as verizonwireless.com, see Figure A-22), or from an online computer company (such as Dell.com). Each type of vendor has its advantages and disadvantages based on the kind of shopping experience you prefer. A brick-and-mortar store provides face-to-face service. A communications store provides the most up-to-date devices for its cellular service. A computer company often provides a wide selection of devices that are compatible with different cellular services.

In addition to purchasing the digital device, you will also need cellular service for the device. You will need to determine the network your digital device can access in order to receive and send data, as well as the price of the data service.

For this Independent Challenge:

1. Use the Internet or any magazines to research the latest offerings in smartphones and tablet computers.

2. Based on your research, list three different smartphones that you like. Be sure to compare the apps and features that come with each smartphone or that are available for each smartphone.

3. Based on your research, list three different tablet computers that you like. Be sure to compare the apps and features that come with each tablet or that are available for each tablet.

4. List the type of network required for each digital device, for example, Wi-Fi, 3G, or 4G. You do not have to understand the differences at this point, just list the type based on your findings.

5. Fill in the following table to help organize your findings.

6. Based on your research, write a concluding paragraph explaining your decision to purchase either a smartphone or a tablet. Support your decision based on your findings.

FIGURE A-22: A communications company that sells smartphones and tablet computers online

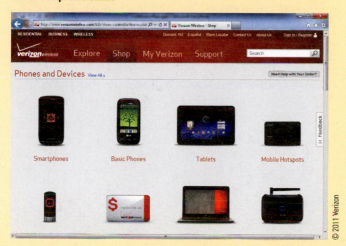

© 2011 Verizon

	Price	Operating system	Display size	Network carrier (Verizon/ AT&T/Other?)	Memory	Weight	Features/ Apps included	Connectivity (Wi-Fi? Bluetooth? 3G? 4G?)
Smartphone								
Tablets								

© Cengage Learning

Guide to Buying a Computer

As you prepare to buy a computer, there are a lot of decisions you have to make. This book is designed to help you build the knowledge base you need to purchase a computer. In this unit, you were introduced to the basics of computing and the Internet. Each subsequent unit covers topics that can help you understand the type of computer you need, the add-on parts you might want to buy, and the software and services that will enhance your computing experience, such as Internet access, software purchases, and so forth. After each unit, you will be asked to answer questions by completing a worksheet. By the end of the book, your Guide to Buying a Computer worksheet will provide comprehensive information about buying a computer.

To help you organize the information you will need when you are ready to buy a computer, you should complete the following activities.

1. Browse through computer magazines such as *Computer Shopper, PC Magazine,* and *Macworld* and online computer stores such as www.dell.com or www.compusa.com (see Figure A-23) to get a general idea of features and prices. Name three magazines and three online resources you reviewed.

   _____

   _____

   _____

2. Computer price points for a basic computer system (system unit, monitor, keyboard, mouse, sound system, Web cam, and printer) can be roughly grouped into three categories.
   * priced higher than $2,000
   * priced between $800 – $2000
   * priced below $800

   Think about how much you want to spend and whether you would be willing to buy older or used technology to meet your budget. Decide on a budget and stick to it. My budget range is _____.

3. Computers can help you perform such a wide variety of tasks that it can be impossible to predict all the ways you might use your new machine. You can, however, make a list of the ways you plan to use your computer and that list can help you think about the features you'll need. Some computer-based activities require more processing or storage capacity than others. If you have some ideas about your computer usage, you're more likely not to have to purchase expensive upgrades for it later.

   Make a list of three ways you plan to use your computer.

   _____

   _____

   _____

FIGURE A-23: A Web site that sells computers

4. As you continue to work through this book, you will learn more about personal computer systems. You will have the opportunity to answer more questions and complete other worksheets with information that will help you when it is time to buy a computer. To get started, fill in this worksheet to complete this portion of the Guide to Buying a Computer worksheet.

Guide to Buying a Computer: Getting started

Questions to consider	Pages where the topic is covered in this book (refer back to these pages to read more about the topic)	Notes (add additional comments, clarifications, or ideas about each topic)
What type of computer do you need?		
Desktop computer		
Portable computer		
If a desktop computer, what kind of case type?		
Tower (vertical)		
Horizontal		
No case (technology as part of flat-panel screen)		
If a portable computer, what kind do you want?		
Notebook		
Tablet		
Netbook		
Which computer platform?		
IBM-compatible PC		
Macintosh		
Will you need access to the Internet and the Web?		
Yes		
No		
Do you plan to email your friends, instructors, or family?		

5. Write any questions you have about buying a computer on the lines that follow. As you continue to work through this book, check back to see if these questions have been answered.

My Questions

_____

_____

_____

_____

Visual Workshop

Today, more and more people use email to communicate. See Figure A-24 for one example of an email message.

To send and receive email, you need an Internet connection, an email account, and software that enables you to compose, read, and delete email messages. An email account consists of an email address, a password, and a mailbox. You can usually obtain an email account from your Internet service provider, your school, or a Web-based email provider, such as Hotmail, Yahoo! Mail, sor Gmail. To get a Hotmail account, you need to get a Windows Live ID.

To access your mail, you need a computer that has an Internet connection. Since Web mail can be accessed from any computer, you can send and receive email from public computers (such as those at a library or in a school lab). You do not need to own a computer. Once you are sure the computer is connected to the Internet, you simply open a browser and type the URL of the Web site that supports the email you signed up for (hotmail.com, yahoo.com, or gmail.com). As soon as you are logged in to your email account, you can begin sending and receiving email.

FIGURE A-24: Using email to communicate

To get a Web-based Gmail account using your own computer, or a public computer if you do not own a computer, just follow these steps.

1. In the Address bar of your browser, enter www.gmail.com.

2. When the Gmail window appears, click the button labeled Create an account.

3. Follow the directions to enter your first name, last name, and login name.

4. Click the check availability button. If the login name you want is already in use, you'll have to try a different one, again clicking the check availability button.

5. When you've selected a valid login name, continue down the page to create a password. Try not to use a name, date, or any dictionary word as your password.

6. Continue down the page to complete the rest of the registration form.

7. Before finalizing your registration, review the information you've entered and jot down your login name and password.

8. Read the Terms of Service, and if you agree, click the I Accept button. That's it! You now have a Gmail account.

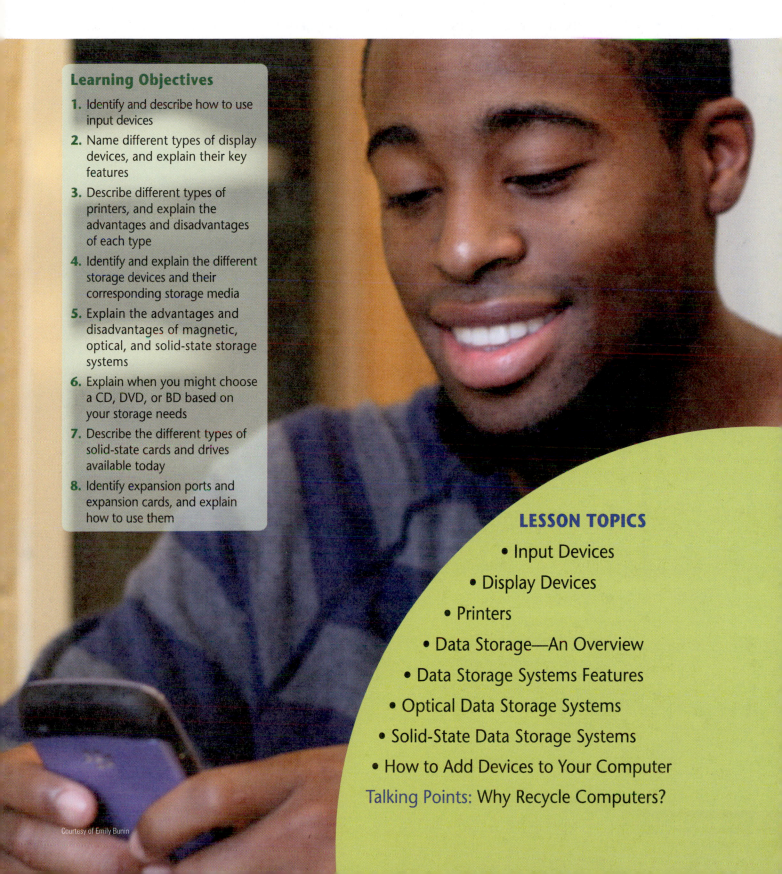

Computer Hardware

Learning Objectives

1. Identify and describe how to use input devices
2. Name different types of display devices, and explain their key features
3. Describe different types of printers, and explain the advantages and disadvantages of each type
4. Identify and explain the different storage devices and their corresponding storage media
5. Explain the advantages and disadvantages of magnetic, optical, and solid-state storage systems
6. Explain when you might choose a CD, DVD, or BD based on your storage needs
7. Describe the different types of solid-state cards and drives available today
8. Identify expansion ports and expansion cards, and explain how to use them

LESSON TOPICS

- Input Devices
- Display Devices
- Printers
- Data Storage—An Overview
- Data Storage Systems Features
- Optical Data Storage Systems
- Solid-State Data Storage Systems
- How to Add Devices to Your Computer

Talking Points: Why Recycle Computers?

Courtesy of Emily Bunin

Input Devices

When you use a computer or any digital device, you need to communicate with it. To tell a computer what to do, you input information. To input the information, you use an input device. An **input device** is computer hardware that can communicate with the computer. Most computer systems include a keyboard and a pointing device, such as a mouse.

Learning Objective 1:
Identify and describe how to use input devices

● **Are all keyboards the same?** Most keyboards are similar. In addition to standard keyboards, you might use on-screen keyboards on smartphones or tablets. See Figure B-1. A computer keyboard includes keys with letters and numbers. It often has keys with characters and special words to control computer-specific tasks. You use the keyboards to input commands, respond to prompts, and type text.

FIGURE B-1: Keyboard examples

on-screen keyboard   built-in keyboard   standard keyboard

© Eldad Carin/iStockphoto   *Courtesy of Hewlett-Packard Company*   *© skaljac/Shutterstock.com*

● **Can I use the keyboard to move around the screen?** Yes, you can use the navigation keypad. See Figure B-2. The navigation keypad includes keys such as the Home, End, and arrow keys. You use these keys to move the **insertion point**

FIGURE B-2: Navigation keys

© skaljac/Shutterstock.com

(also called the **cursor**) on the screen. An insertion point indicates where the characters you type will appear. The insertion point typically looks like a flashing vertical bar on the screen. You can change the location of the insertion point by pressing the navigation keys or by clicking a **pointing device**, such as a mouse.

● **Why do I need a mouse?** Often, you will find that it is easier to use a mouse to give some commands to a computer than it is to use a keyboard. A **mouse** allows you to control an on-screen pointer. A standard desktop computer uses a mouse as its primary pointing device. You can also use a mouse with many notebook computers. A typical mouse, shown in Figure B-3, includes one or more buttons.

FIGURE B-3: Typical mouse features

Scroll wheel

Left mouse button

Additional buttons

Right mouse button

Used with permission from Microsoft

● **How do I use a mouse?** You use a mouse by sliding a mouse along a hard surface. Some people use a mouse pad. As you move the mouse, a pointer on the screen moves. If you move the mouse to the left, the pointer on the screen moves to the left. In addition, you click the buttons on the mouse to give commands to the computer. Some mice have extra buttons for additional actions. For example, a scroll wheel can be used to scroll up or down a window. An extra button in the left side of the mouse can be pressed to undo a command. See Table B-1 for common mouse actions.

● **How do mice communicate with the computer?** Some mice are connected to a computer with a cable or wire. These wired mice communicate with the computer through the cable. Other mice are wireless. Wireless mice communicate with the computer using radio signals. Many people prefer wireless mice because there is no cable to get tangled in when they move the mouse.

For both wired and wireless mice, you have several choices. An **optical mouse** uses an LED (an electronic light) and computer chip to track your mouse movements as a light beam bounces off a hard surface, such as a desk. A **laser mouse** uses a laser as the light source to track mouse movement. Both provide the flexibility to use the mouse on a wide variety of surfaces without a mouse pad.

● **What other pointing devices can I use?** Other pointing devices include touchpads, trackballs, and pointing sticks. These devices are typically used with notebook computers and other mobile devices and smartphones as an alternative to a mouse. A **touchpad**, also called a **trackpad**, is a touch-sensitive surface on which you can slide your fingers to move the on-screen pointer. See Figure B-4. A **trackball** is a roller ball on the top of a mouse. You use your fingers or the palm of your hand to roll the ball and move the pointer. A pointing stick, or TrackPoint, looks like the tip of an eraser embedded in the keyboard of a notebook computer. You can push the TrackPoint up, down, or sideways to move the on-screen pointer.

FIGURE B-4: Other pointing devices

Touchpad on a notebook

Trackpad on a smartphone

● **Why do some computers have touch screens?** Many smartphones and other mobile devices, tablet computers, and information kiosks use a touch screen. Special software works to accept the touch screen input.

Touch screen technology can interpret a single touch or more complex input, such as handwriting. You cycle through screens by swiping the glass. You zoom in and out by pinching and expanding two fingers. You rotate objects by twisting two fingers. Some touch screens use a stylus to provide input. See Figure B-5. Be sure to use the stylus intended for your touch screen because touch screens can be damaged by sharp objects.

FIGURE B-5: Touch screen examples

● **What if I want to input something I created on paper?** If you have data that exists on paper, you can use a **scanner** to input that data. The scanner captures the image, picture, or text and creates a digital graphics file.

● **Can I enter data by speaking?** Yes, a microphone is an input device that converts spoken words or sound information into a digital format. There are speech-to-text programs that can accept sound as input, which allows you to create a text file from the spoken words. Also, if you use your computer as an Internet telephone, you speak into a microphone and the telephone program sends it through the computer to the person you are speaking with.

● **Are digital cameras input devices?** Yes, a digital camera, creates photographic images as files. A web cam and a digital video camera capture moving images and sound as files. Image and video files can be transferred from a digital camera to any computer. Once these images or videos are on a computer, you can view, play, or change the images.

TABLE B-1: Common mouse actions

Action and result	How you do it
Click to select an object	Press the left mouse button once, and then immediately release it.
Double-click to activate an object	Press the left mouse button twice in rapid succession without moving the body of the mouse.
Right-click to display a shortcut menu	Press the right mouse button once, and then immediately release it.
Drag to move an object	Hold the left mouse button down while you move the mouse.

© Cengage Learning

Display Devices

UNIT B Concepts

While working on a computer, you will want to see what's going on. You need to look at the data as you input it. You also want to look at the output. A display system is the main output device for a computer. Two key components of a computer display system are a display device or screen and a graphics card.

> ## Learning Objective 2:
> Name different types of display devices, and explain their key features

● **What is a display device?** A **display device** is the computer hardware that shows, or displays, the data. It shows the input as you enter data. It shows the output once the data has been processed. The main display device for a computer is either a monitor or a screen. Smartphones, tablet computers, and other mobile devices have screens.

● **Are a monitor and a screen the same thing?** Many people use the terms *monitor* and *screen* interchangeably, but they are not technically the same thing. A monitor is a stand-alone display device that connects to a computer. A screen is the area where output is displayed. A desktop computer has a monitor with a screen. A notebook, netbook, and tablet computer, as well as other mobile devices such as a smartphone, each have a screen.

● **What are my choices for a display device?** Two technologies are commonly used for computer display devices: LCD and LED. See Figure B-6. Your computer monitor will most likely have an **LCD (liquid crystal display)** screen. LCD monitors are also called flat-panel displays. LCD monitors produce an image by manipulating light within a layer of liquid crystal cells. The advantages of an LCD monitor include display clarity, low

radiation emission, portability, and compactness. Stand-alone LCD monitors are available for desktop computers. LCD screens are standard equipment for notebook computers. An LED (light emitting diodes) screen looks similar to an LCD screen but it uses light emitting diodes for the backlighting. LEDs are considered more environmentally friendly than LCDs.

● **What type of screen do mobile devices use?** Mobile devices such as mobile phones, portable media players, GPS devices, and digital cameras, use **OLED (organic light emitting diodes)** or LCD technology. See Figure B-7. Each technology has its advantages. For example, an OLED display device draws less power than an LCD screen. OLEDs have a crisp image and a fast response rate. OLED screens work well in direct sunlight. The image on an OLED screen can be seen from any angle.

FIGURE B-7: Display technology for smartphones

Example of an OLED screen   Example of an LCD screen

● **What is a graphics card?** A graphics card is the another important component of your display system. A **graphics card** contains the technology used to display images on the screen. It also contains special memory, which stores images as they are processed but before they are displayed. The amount of available memory is the key to the overall performance, including response rate, of the display system.

FIGURE B-6: Examples of monitors

LCD

LED

- **What is response rate?** **Response rate** is how fast a screen updates the information being displayed. Display devices with fast response rates display a crisp image with minimal blurring or "ghosting" of moving objects. Response rate is an important factor for fast action games, 3D modeling, and graphics-intensive desktop publishing.

- **Where is the graphics card?** A graphics card can be built into a computer's motherboard or plugged into the motherboard. The graphics card is a chip built into the motherboard of a notebook or tablet computer, as well as other mobile devices.

- **What does a graphics card do?** Think of the computer screen as a grid. The rows and columns make cells in the grid. A graphics card sends an image to the screen to fill the grid. The graphics card sends the image at a specific resolution. **Resolution** is the maximum number of horizontal and vertical pixels displayed on the screen. A **pixel (picture element)** is a single point or the smallest unit in a graphic image. Each pixel fills one cell of the grid. As resolutions increase, the computer displays a larger work area on the screen with text and other objects appearing smaller. See Figure B-8. You can set the resolution on a Windows PC using options in the Control Panel. Higher resolutions are possible if your graphics card has enough memory to support those resolutions and if your display device is capable of displaying those resolutions.

- **Does it matter if my display device is square or rectangular?** No, but you should use a resolution that works best for your display device. Some monitors look square. For these monitors, a resolution based on a 4:3 aspect ratio works best. The 4:3 ratio matches the monitor since the width is slightly larger than the height. Some monitors have a rectangle shape. These are widescreen monitors. For widescreen monitors, a resolution based on a 16:9 aspect ratios works best.

- **What other factors besides resolution affect image quality?** In addition to resolution, image quality is determined by screen size, dot pitch, and color depth. These factors are all controlled by the graphics card.

- **What is screen size?** **Screen size** is the measurement in inches from one corner of the screen diagonally across to the opposite corner. Although large screens exist for commercial use, typical computer monitor screen sizes range from 15" to more than 20". In addition to screen size, you should also consider a monitor's **viewing angle width**, which indicates how far to the side you can still clearly see the screen image. A wide viewing angle indicates that you can view the screen from various positions without compromising image quality. A 170 degree viewing angle is preferable to a viewing angle of 150 degrees.

- **What is dot pitch?** **Dot pitch (dp)** is a measure of image clarity. A smaller dot pitch means a crisper image. Unlike resolution, dot pitch is not customizable. A display device's specifications include dot pitch.

- **What is color depth?** The number of colors that a monitor and graphics card can display is referred to as **color depth** or **bit depth**. Most PCs are capable of displaying millions of colors and photographic-quality images. On a Windows PC, you can change the color setting to customize the color depth by using options in the Control Panel.

- **Can I watch TV on my display device?** Yes, if your display system is equipped with NTSC (National TV Standards Committee) or HDTV (high-definition television) circuitry. Display devices rated for 1080i or 1080p are compatible with HDTV standards. Television signals are sent to the computer through an antenna or cable. You can even view computer data and television on the same display device at the same time using split-screen or picture-in-picture format.

FIGURE B-8: Comparing screen resolutions

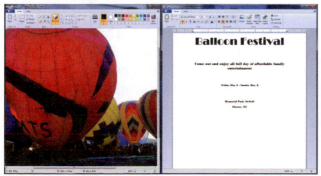

High resolution
Text and images fill the screen and more content can fit on a screen with a higher resolution.

Low resolution
Text and images appear larger but less content can fit on a screen with a lower resolution.

Printers

Most output is viewed using a display device. This output is called **soft copy**. Sometimes, you want the output on paper. To create printed copy, you use a printer. Printed output is called **hard copy**. You can print hard copy on different media, such as paper, labels, or transparencies. Printers differ in resolution and speed, both of which affect the print quality and price. To find a printer that meets your needs, it is important to understand the different types of printers and their features.

> **Learning Objective 3:**
> Describe different types of printers, and explain the advantages and disadvantages of each type

● **What are the most common types of printers in use today?** The most common types of printers in use today are either ink-jet printers or laser printers. Both ink-jet printers and laser printers have features in common. For example, both are available as black and white or color printers. Both have trays for different paper sizes. You can print on 8" × 11" paper, 8" × 14" paper, envelopes, postcards, transparencies, and more. Both types of printers also have drawbacks to consider. For example, cost over the life of the printer, as well as the speed at which the printer produces hard copy.

● **How does an ink-jet printer work?** An **ink-jet printer** has a print head that sprays ink onto paper to form characters and graphics. Ink-jet printers usually use two cartridges: a black ink cartridge and a color cartridge that holds colored inks. See Figure B-9. Most ink-jet printers are small, lightweight, and inexpensive, yet produce very good-quality color output. However, the ink cartridges can be expensive and can add to the overall cost of printing.

FIGURE B-9: An ink jet printer

Color ink cartridges

Paper tray

Black ink cartridge

Courtesy of Hewlett-Packard Company

● **How does a laser printer work?** A **laser printer** uses a technology that produces dots of light on a light-sensitive drum. Instead of ink cartridges, laser printers use **toner** cartridges. See Figure B-10. Toner is the fine powder that is applied to the drum, and then creates the image on the paper. Laser printers are popular for situations that require high-volume output or good-quality printouts. Laser printers are generally more expensive than ink-jet printers.

FIGURE B-10: A laser printer

Toner cartridge

Paper tray

Courtesy of Hewlett-Packard Company

● **What determines the quality of the printed images?** **Printer resolution** determines the quality or sharpness of printed images and text. Resolution is measured by the number of dots printed per linear inch, or **dots per inch (dpi)**. At normal reading distance, a resolution of about 900 dots per inch appears solid to the human eye. At 900 dpi, if you look closely, a dot pattern will be evident. Good-quality printers are rated from 2400 to 4800 dpi. If you want the printed images to have the quality of professionally printed books, use a printer with a resolution of 2400 dpi or higher.

● **How can I know if a printer is fast?** You can look at the pages per minute (ppm) and memory specifications provided by the manufacturer. Printer speed is measured by the number of **pages per minute (ppm)** output. Color printouts typically take longer to print than black-and-white printouts. Pages that contain mostly text tend to print faster than pages that contain graphics. Most printers for personal or small business use are rated from 15 to 30 ppm.

Memory capacity is another factor to consider when evaluating printer speed. Printers often work in the background while you work on other computer tasks. If your printer has lots of memory, you can send many print jobs to the printer. The print jobs will be in the printer's memory and not in your computer's memory. More memory is required to print color images and documents with graphics. You can work more efficiently if your printer has more memory.

- **Can a printer print on both sides of a page in one pass?** Yes, a **duplex printer** can print on both sides of the paper. This environment-friendly option saves paper. However, duplex printing slows down the print process on ink-jet printers because they have to pause to let the ink dry before printing the second side.

- **Does the number of pages I print affect the life of my printer? Duty cycle** determines how many pages a printer is able to print in a specified period of time. A printer's duty cycle is usually measured in pages per month. For example, on average, a personal laser printer has a duty cycle of about 3000 pages per month—that means roughly 100 pages per day. However, you wouldn't want to use it to produce 3,000 pages on one day. You can print more pages than the specified duty cycle, but this could shorten the usability of your printer. Also, a printer with a higher duty cycle will have a shorter useful life.

- **How does a printer connect to my computer?** A printer connects to your computer using one of the following connection options: USB port, serial port, parallel port, or network port. Usually a cable is used to connect a printer to a computer. However, a printer can also connect to a computer wirelessly if the printer and computer both have the wireless technology needed to connect.

You can connect a printer directly to your personal computer and use it only with that computer. But, sometimes, you might want to use a printer with more than one computer.

- **How do I use a printer with more than one computer?** If your computers are part of a LAN (local area network), you can share your printer with the other computers. In this situation, each computer on the network sends its print jobs to your computer's printer for output. This allows many computers to share one resource, the printer.

    Another way to configure network printing for multiple users is to purchase a **network-enabled printer** that connects directly to the network, rather than to one of the computers on a network. The network connection can be wired or wireless.

- **Do I need a different printer to print lots of photographs?** Yes, for more professional output, you want to use a **photo printer**. These printers have slower output speeds when compared to ink-jet or laser printers, but they do produce professional-quality images on specialized papers.

- **How do I know which type of printer is best for me?** The type of printer you need depends on several factors. For example: Do you need black and white hard copy or color hard copy Do you often need to print a lot of pages at one time? Are you working with a stand-alone or a networked computer? Do you want a wired or a wireless printer? Once you know the answers to these questions, you will know what type of printer best meets your needs.

Options for printing your photos

Do you print a lot of photographs? If so, you should compare the cost of printing the photographs using your printer to the cost of printing the photographs commercially. You can often have digital images printed over the Web using online services, such as Kodak Gallery, Snapfish, or Flickr. The printed photos are then mailed to you. You can also take the digital image files on a disc or flash drive to a store and have the photographs printed there. You can often shop while you wait for your photos. Some stores allow you to upload images to their Web site, where you specify your printing preferences, and then pick up the photos at your local store. Some stores even have self-service stations in the store. See Figure B-11. These printing services usually allow you to edit your digital images, for example, to remove red-eye or to crop an unwanted object out of the image. If you consider the cost of paper and ink to print large quantities of photographs, these services often are more economical. But for occasional use, a photo-printer provides quality images at a reasonable cost.

FIGURE B-11: Self-service photo printing

Courtesy of Hewlett-Packard Company

Data Storage—An Overview

As you use a computer, you will want to store or save your work. Once stored, you can use your work again or share it with other people. When you store your work, you save it using storage technology. The term **storage technology** refers to data storage systems that make it possible for a computer or digital device to store and retrieve data.

Learning Objective 4:
Identify and explain the different storage devices and their corresponding storage media

● **What is a data storage system?** A data storage system is made up of two main parts: a storage device and a storage medium. A **storage device** is the equipment that stores and retrieves data from its storage medium. Storage devices include hard drives, card readers, tape drives, flash drives, CD drives, DVD drives, BD drives, and solid-state card readers. A **storage medium** is the technology that holds data. Storage media include hard drives, tape, memory cards, flash drives, CDs, DVDs, and BDs. Refer to Figure B-12 for examples of storage devices and storage media.

FIGURE B-12: Examples of storage devices and storage media

Top, left: © Dmitry Rukhlenko/Shutterstock.com; © Ruslan Ivantsov/Shutterstock.com; © Tatiana Popova/Shutterstock.com; Kingston Technology Company, Inc.; Top, right: Kingston Technology Company, Inc.; BiTMICRO Networks, Inc.

● **Are the storage medium and the storage device always two separate parts?** No. Some data storage systems are self-contained, while others are two distinct parts. For example, a hard drive is both the storage device and the storage medium. A USB flash drive is both a storage device and the storage medium. But, a CD/DVD drive is a storage device and it uses CDs or DVDs as the storage media. And, a flash card reader is a storage device and it uses solid state cards as its storage media.

● **What is the main data storage system for a personal computer system?** The main storage system for a personal computer is a **hard drive**. Hard drives can be internal (permanently installed inside the system unit), removable, or external. Hard drives can be mechanical or use **solid-state technology**. Mechanical drives have moving parts. **Solid-state drives (SSD)** have no moving parts. The terms hard drive and hard disk drive are often used interchangeably.

● **Why are hard drives so popular?** Hard drives are the preferred type of main storage for most computer systems. They provide lots of storage, fast access to data, and are inexpensive. Most computers come with an internal hard drive that is installed in the computer and cannot be moved easily from one computer to another. You may not know what a hard drive looks like because it is usually found inside the system unit. Personal computer hard drive platters are typically 3½" in diameter with storage capacities ranging from 60 GB to over 2 TB. Refer to Figure B-13 to see what a mechanical hard drive looks like. Tablet computers, mobile devices, and some notebooks use a solid-state non-removable internal hard drive.

Spindle   Read-write head   Platter

What other storage devices can I use with my personal computer?

In addition to the hard drive just discussed, you can use additional storage devices such as CD/DVD/BD drives, USB flash drives, solid-state drives, and solid-state card readers.

Why would I want to use different storage devices?

Storage devices, such as hard drives, provide fast access to data. Some storage devices, such as CDs DVDs, and BVDs, are more dependable than others. Some storage devices, such as solid-state storage **USB flash drives** and external hard drives, are portable and can be moved easily from one computer to another computer.

How do these storage devices connect to my computer?

The system unit case for a desktop computer contains several storage device "parking spaces" called **drive bays** or **expansion bays**. Storage devices are installed in these drive bays. These bays are typically hidden from view with a faceplate. See Figure B-14. When you buy a computer, you will need to find out how many drive bays the computer has and what type of storage devices can be connected to the computer using the drive bay(s). Any drive that is mounted inside the system unit and that uses removable media or that has to

FIGURE B-14: Drive bays

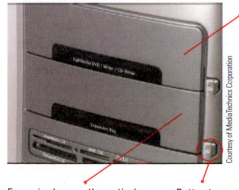

DVD writer/CD writer drive

Expansion bay; another optical drive can be added here

Button to open drive

be controlled manually by pushing a button or inserting the media into a slot, such as a CD/DVD/BD drive, must be able to be accessed from outside the system unit.

What if my computer doesn't have any empty drive bays?

In this case, you will want to add an external storage device. Some storage devices such as an external hard drive, a USB flash drive, or a card reader connect to your computer using a USB port. If you do not have enough USB ports for all the devices you want to connect, then you can use a USB hub. A USB hub adds ports to your computer, as shown in Figure B-15.

FIGURE B-15: Drives connected through a USB hub

USB flash drives

Self-powered USB hub

External hard drive

Courtesy of MediaTechnics Corporation

How do I connect storage devices to my notebook, netbook, and tablet computers?

These computers do not have drive bays. You will want to connect storage devices to these computers using an available USB port or a USB hub.

How can I increase my storage capacity?

You can increase the storage capacity of your computer by adding a second internal hard drive to an empty drive bay. You can also add an external hard drive that connects via a USB port.

Is my data safe on the hard drive?

In general, yes. But keep in mind that the read-write heads in a mechanical hard drive hover a microscopic distance above the disk surface. A head crash might happen if a read-write head runs into dirt on the disk or if the hard drive is jarred while it is in use. A head crash will damage some or all of the data on the disk. To help prevent dirt from contacting the platters and causing head crashes, a hard drive is sealed in its case. Although hard drives have become considerably more rugged in recent years, you should still handle and transport them with care.

Is there a hard drive in my iPod and other mobile devices?

Yes, although the physical sizes of the hard drives vary. Mobile devices use a miniature hard drive (sometimes called a microdrive). For example Apple's current iPod uses a 1.8" drive that can store 30 to 160 GB.

Data Storage Systems Features

Data storage systems for personal computers use magnetic, optical, or solid-state technology. Data storage systems can be compared based on their versatility, durability, capacity, and speed.

Learning Objective 5:
Explain the advantages and disadvantages of magnetic, optical, and solid-state storage systems

● **Why do I need versatility in a data storage system?** Most likely you will be working with other people. You will want to be able to store data on your storage medium and then give that storage medium to another person. That person can then use the storage medium to access the data. Or, you may have to use different computers. To move data among different computers, you will want data storage systems that are versatile. Some storage devices can access data from only one type of medium. More versatile storage devices can access data from several different media. For example, a DVD drive can access data on these storage media: DVDs, DVD movies, audio CDs, data CDs, and CD-Rs. A USB flash drive can plug into any USB port. Both a DVD and a flash drive are versatile.

● **Why do I need a data storage system that is durable?** Do you travel or carry your data files with you? If so, then you need a storage system that is durable. Most data storage systems can be damaged by mishandling them or by heat and moisture. Optical and solid-state technologies are more durable than magnetic technologies. They do not damage easily. This helps you prevent data loss. Solid-state storage devices are the most durable at this time.

● **Why is storage capacity important?** Different data storage systems hold different amounts of data. **Storage capacity** is the maximum amount of data (documents, photographs, songs, video) that can be stored on a storage medium. Storage capacity is measured in kilobytes (KB), megabytes (MB), gigabytes (GB), or terabytes (TB). Graphics and video require more storage capacity than text. You need more storage for photographs and video than you need for your school reports or letters. Before deciding on a data storage system, you need to be sure the data storage systems you use can hold all the data you need to store.

● **Do different data storage systems access and transfer data at different speeds?** Yes. There are two factors to take into account when considering access speed: access time and data transfer rate. **Access time** is the average time it takes a computer to locate data on the storage medium and read it. Access time is measured in **milliseconds** (thousandths of a second, abbreviated as **ms**). **Data transfer rate** is the amount of data that a storage device can move from the storage medium to the computer per second. So, if you are watching a movie on your computer, you want the fastest data transfer rate possible.

● **What does random access mean? Random access** (also called **direct access**) is the ability of a device to jump directly to the requested data. Hard drives, solid-state drives, CD drives, DVD drives, and BD drives are random-access devices. A tape drive, used with some business computers for long-term storage, must use slower **sequential access**, which means it reads through the data from the beginning of the tape to the end. As a result, accessing data on a tape is much slower than accessing data on a hard drive. The advantage of random access becomes clear when you consider how much faster and easier it is to locate a song on a CD (random access) or MP3 player (random access solid-state storage) than on tape (sequential access).

● **Which data storage systems use magnetic storage technology?** Hard drives and tapes use magnetic storage. **Magnetic storage** stores data by magnetizing microscopic particles on the disk or tape surface. The particles retain their magnetic orientation until that orientation is changed. Patterns of magnetized particles are interpreted as the 0s and 1s that represent data. Data stored magnetically can be changed or deleted simply by altering the magnetic orientation of the appropriate particles on the disk surface. Refer to Figure B-16.

Randomly scattered particles   Magnetized particles   Read-write head   Disk surface

© Cengage Learning

● **Which storage systems use optical storage technology?** CDs, DVDs, and BDs use optical storage technologies. **Optical storage** stores data as microscopic light and dark spots on the disc surface. Low-power laser light is used to read the data stored on an optical disc. Patterns of light and dark are interpreted as the 1s and 0s that represent data. Figure B-17 shows the layers that make up an optical disc. You use an optical storage system because its storage media (CDs, DVDs, and BDs) are easy to transport and fairly durable. However, CDs, DVDs, and BDs do still require some special handling in order to be sure that data stored on these optical media is not lost or damaged due to environmental conditions or poor handling.

FIGURE B-17: Optical storage

Polycarbonate substrate
Reflective layer
Recording layer 1
Spacer layer
Semitransparent reflective layer

Laser beams   Recording layer 0   Polycarbonate substrate

© Cengage Learning

● **Which data storage systems use solid-state storage technology?** Some hard drives, a variety of compact storage cards (also called memory cards or memory sticks) and flash drives (also called thumb drives or jump sticks) use solid-state technology. **Solid-state storage** technology stores data in a durable, erasable, low-power chip. Solid-state storage technology provides faster access to data than magnetic or optical storage technology because it includes no moving parts. Very little power is required, which makes solid-state storage ideal for battery-operated devices, such as a digital camera. Solid-state storage is very durable—it is usually not affected by vibrations, magnetic fields, or extreme temperature fluctuations—and very portable. Flash drives have become trendy stylish items that can be fun to carry. They can even be worn as a fashion accessory. See Figure B-18.

FIGURE B-18: A flash drive can take many fun forms

Left: © Fazakas Mihaly/Shutterstock Right, top: © andsem/iStockphoto;
© Hasloo Group Production Studio/Shutterstock.com

● **What is tape storage? Tape storage** technology consists of a tape drive for the storage device and a tape for the storage medium. Tape drives are available in either internal or external models. The most popular types of tape drives for personal computers use tape cartridges for the storage medium. A **tape cartridge** is a removable magnetic tape module similar to a cassette tape. Tape storage is used mainly for back-up storage today, most often for backing up business or professional systems.

Non-technical words used to describe using a data storage system

You use certain words to describe what happens when you use a data storage system. When you want to retrieve data, you say the storage device is "reading," "loading," or "opening" a file. The storage device reads the file on the storage medium and loads the information into RAM. Once the file is loaded, it is open and ready for you to use. "Ripping" is the term used to describe copying files from CDs, DVDs, and BDs onto your hard drive. For CDs, DVDs, and BDs, you often use the term "burning" to describe when files are copied to a disc.

Optical Data Storage Systems

You may have used a CD to listen to music. You may have used a DVD or a Blu-ray Disc (BD) to watch a movie. But did you know you can also use these media to store computer data? **CDs (compact discs)**, **DVDs (digital video disc** or **digital versatile disc)**, and **BDs (Blu-ray Discs)** use optical storage technologies. Optical storage media use one of three technologies: read-only (ROM), recordable (R), or rewritable (RW).

Learning Objective 6:
Explain when you might choose a CD, DVD, or BD based on your storage needs

● **What are the parts of an optical storage system?** An optical storage system consists of a drive and the storage media used in that drive. The rest of this lesson provides more information about the types of optical drives available, as well as the type of storage media each drive can use.

● **What is the main difference between CD, DVD, and BD?** Today, most computers come equipped with one or more drives designed to work with CD, DVD, or BD discs. The basic difference between these technologies is the amount of data each disc can store. Current CD standards have the capacity to store 80 minutes of music or 700 MB of data. DVD standards offer 4.7 GB (4,700 MB) of data storage, about seven times as much capacity as a CD. A double layer DVD has two recordable layers on the same side and can store 8.5 GB of data. Currently, BDs have the highest storage capacity for optical storage media. They offer 25 GB capacity per layer. A double layer BD disc holds 50 GB of data.

● **What do the extra letters after CD, DVD, and BD mean?** The extra letters associated with a CD, DVD, or BD help you recognize how you can use the disc. Using CD as an example:

  ■ CD-ROM means read-only technology. A computer CD-ROM, DVD-ROM, or BD-ROM disc contains data that was stamped on the disc surface when it was manufactured, such as commercial software, music, and movies. Data cannot be added, changed, or deleted from CD-ROM, DVD-ROM, or BD-ROM discs.

  ■ CD-R means CD **recordable technology**. If you need to write data to the storage media, then you need to purchase recordable discs. You can usually write to a CD-R disc in multiple sessions. For example, you can store two files on a CD-R disc today, and add data for a few more files to the disc at a later time. This is also true for DVD-R/DVD+R and BD-R discs.

  ■ CD-RW means CD **rewritable technology**. If you need to write to the disc and rewrite to the disc, then you need to purchase the rewritable (multiple session use) discs. When you use these discs, you can record and erase stored data multiple times, which makes this a flexible storage option. This is also true for DVD-RW/DVD+RW. For Blu-ray Discs, you would look for BD-RE discs. BD-RE can be erased and re-recorded multiple times.

● **What type of optical disc should I buy?** When you purchase optical discs, be sure to purchase the type that works in your computer system's optical drive and meets your storage needs. To be able to write to the disc, you would need either the R or RW/RE format.

Understanding hard drive partitions

A hard drive partition is a section of a hard drive that is treated as a separate storage device. Many computers are configured with a single hard drive partition that contains the operating system, programs, and data. Some new computers come with two partitions. It is even possible to partition external hard drives. Partitions appear as independent hard drives but they are one physical drive in your computer. When you look at the single drive using Windows Explorer, each partition is labeled separately (such as C drive and D drive), These are sometimes called logical drives. The main partition is often labeled OS (C:), and it contains the operating system and other program and data files. The default folders for Windows are on the C drive. The second partition is often labeled Recovery (D):. This partition contains files that can be used to help restore the computer if drive C malfunctions. Partitions are not the same as folders. Partitions are more permanent, and a special utility is required to create, modify, or delete them.

● **Should my computer system have a CD, DVD, or BD drive?** Yes, it is a good idea to have a **CD drive**, a **DVD drive**, or a **BD drive**. You need to know your storage needs to know which type of optical disc drive is best for you. The most versatile, and at the moment the most expensive, optical storage device is a Blu-ray Disc writer/DVD writer. Optical drives can be built into your computer or you can use external optical drives that connect through USB ports. External optical drives can be moved as needed among your computers.

● **How do I insert a disc into an optical drive?** First, you must open the drive. Usually there is button that you push. When you push the button the drawer slides out. See Figure B-19. You hold the disc on the sides and place it in the drawer so the label or printed description of the disc is facing up. After the disc is set in the drawer, gently push the drawer or press the button and the drawer will close.

● **Can I use a CD, DVD, or BD drive instead of a hard drive?** No. A rewritable CD, DVD, or BD drive is a fine addition to a computer system, but it is not a replacement for a hard drive. Unfortunately, the process of reading data from and writing data to a rewritable disc is relatively slow compared to hard drive access speed. In addition, the storage capacity of CDs and DVDs is much less than the storage capacity of hard drives.

● **How does the optical drive work?** Figure B-20 illustrates how a CD drive works. Optical drives contain a spindle that rotates the disc over a laser lens. The laser directs a beam of light toward the underside of the disc. As the drive reads the disc, the light's reflections are translated into the 0s and 1s that represent data. Blu-ray Disc technology uses blue-violet colored lasers to read data. DVD technology uses a red laser. CD technology uses a near infrared laser.

FIGURE B-20: How an optical drive works

Courtesy of MediaTechnics Corporation

Tracking mechanism positions a disc track over the laser lens

Laser lens directs a beam of light to the underside of the CD-ROM disc

Laser pickup assembly senses the reflections and translates the information into 1s and 0s

Drive spindle spins disc

FIGURE B-19: Inserting a disc in an optical drive

Courtesy of MediaTechnics Corporation

Viewing your data storage systems using Windows Explorer

All of the data storage systems connected to your computer are named. You can view the data storage systems connected to your computer using a file management system, such as Windows Explorer. To view the contents of a disc or any media in Windows Explorer, open Windows Explorer and then click Computer to see all of the storage devices connected to your computer, including any external hard drives, any optical drives such as CD, DVD, or BD drives, any solid state drives such as flash drives, even cameras that you connect through a USB cable, and any network drives. Select the drive to see the contents in the right pane of the window. See Figure B-21.

FIGURE B-21: Viewing data storage systems connected to a computer

Used with permission from Microsoft

Solid-State Data Storage Systems

Have you ever used a cell phone? A digital camera? An MP3 player? If you have, then you have also used solid-state data storage. Solid-state data storage is portable and durable. It provides fast access to data, offers high-capacity storage, and uses very little power. It is an ideal solution for storing data on mobile devices and transporting data from one device to another.

> **Learning Objective 7:**
> Describe the different types of solid-state cards and drives available today

● **When would I use solid-state storage?** Solid-state storage systems are suitable for many storage needs. See Figure B-22.

FIGURE B-22: Examples of solid state storage media

Used mainly in cameras

Used mainly in mobile devices, such as GPS devices, MP3 players, PDAs

Used for portable storage through a USB connection

Used for portable storage through a USB connection; larger storage capacity than a flash drive

Used inside a computer for permanent storage

Counter-clockwise from top left: Courtesy of MediaTechnics Corporation; Courtesy of MediaTechnics Corporation; Courtesy of MediaTechnics Corporation; © Oleksiy Mark/Shutterstock.com; Courtesy of Iomega

You might use a solid-state memory card in your digital camera. A solid-state memory card in a digital camera can store hundreds of pictures. You can remove the card from the camera and insert it into a card reader that is connected to a computer. Once the card is connected to your computer, you can transfer the files to your hard drive so the photos can be edited using the computer's graphics software and transmitted via the computer's Internet connection.

You might use a solid-state memory card in your MP3 player. You can download MP3 music files using your computer and then store the files on a solid-state memory card. Next, you can insert the card into a portable MP3 player so you can hear your favorite tunes while you are on the go.

You might use solid-state storage, such as a flash drive or an external solid-state drive, for your portable computing needs, that is, for transporting data from one computer to another.

● **Why is solid-state storage so popular?** Solid-state storage uses a technology that stores data in a nonvolatile, erasable,

low-power chip. A **chip** is an electronic circuit. You will learn more about chips later in this book. Very little power is required to store the data. Solid-state storage is ideal for battery-operated devices, such as digital cameras or smartphones. Once the data is stored, the chip retains the data without the need for an external power source.

● **How do I know which solid-state cards to buy?** The type of card you buy depends on the device it will be used with. There are over 50 types of flash cards available. The device you buy should indicate the cards you can use with that device. Examples of several types of solid-state memory cards are shown in Figure B-23. The formats for these small, flat cards include CompactFlash (CF), Memory Sticks, Secure Digital (SD), Secure Digital High Capacity (SDHC), Micro SD, Micro SDHC, and Secure Digital Extended Capacity (SDXC). The micro cards are used in smartphones and portable media players.

FIGURE B-23: Solid state cards

Courtesy of Kingston Technology Company, Inc.

■ **CompactFlash (CF) cards** are about the size of a matchbook and provide high storage capacities and access speeds. CompactFlash cards include a built-in controller that reads data from and writes data to the card. CompactFlash cards use a card reader to transfer data from the card to your computer; the built-in controller tells the card reader what to do. With their high storage capacities and access speeds, CompactFlash cards are ideal for use on high-end digital cameras that require megabytes of storage for each photo.

- **SecureDigital (SD) cards** are popular for digital images and MP3 storage. They use a card reader to copy data from the card to a computer. Newer SDHC cards have 32 GB maximum capacity; SDXC cards have a 2 TB maximum capacity. Although SDHC and SDXC cards fit in a standard SD slot, older devices might not be able to handle such high storage capacities.

- **Memory stick** technology was originally developed by Sony. Memory sticks are now developed in a joint venture with SanDisk. They have been expanded to include extended high capacity formats. Some can reach 2 TB of storage with very fast data transfer rates.

● **Will my computer be able to read my solid-state storage cards?** Solid-state storage cards require a device called a **card reader** to transfer data to or from a computer. A card reader can be built into a computer's system unit. Refer to Figure B-24. Sometimes referred to as 5-in-1, 7-in-1, or all-in-one card readers, these combination devices work with multiple types of solid-state storage formats. If your computer has one of these readers, it will be able to read your solid-state storage cards.

FIGURE B-24: Card reader built into a system unit

Memory card

5-in-1 card reader

● **What if my computer system does not have a built-in card reader?** You can use a stand-alone card reader. See Figure B-25. A stand-alone card reader usually connects to a computer via USB. To connect the stand-alone card reader to your computer, simply plug the USB cable into an available USB port.

FIGURE B-25: Stand–alone card reader

Courtesy of Kingston Technology Company, Inc.

● **Do I always need a card reader to read solid-state storage?** No. USB flash drives and solid-state drives (SSD) (see Figure B-26) incorporate the memory and the reader into one device. Each has a built-in connector that plugs directly into a computer's port. USB flash drives plug into a USB port and internal solid-state drives plug into the motherboard. External USB solid-state flash drives that connect via a USB port are also available. SSDs have no moving parts so they are more durable than mechanical hard drives.

FIGURE B-26: Examples of solid-state drives

From left: © Albert Lozano/ Shutterstock.com; BitMICRO Networks, Inc.; Courtesy of Apricorn

Flash drive   Internal solid-state   External solid-state
               hard drive   hard drive

● **What is the best choice for portability?** USB flash drives are easy to take from one computer to another. When connected to your computer's USB port, you can open, edit, delete, and run files stored on a USB flash drive just as if though those files were stored on your computer's hard drive. USB flash drives are about the size of a large paperclip and so durable that you can literally carry them on your key ring. They are usually called flash drives, thumb drives, or jump sticks. They are also nicknamed pen drives, keychain drives, or UFDs (Universal Flash Drive). They come in a variety of shapes and sizes. Some samples were shown previously in Figure B-18.

How to Add Devices to Your Computer

You can expand or improve the capability of your computer by adding computer peripherals. Some peripherals you might want to add include a scanner, a different mouse, a joystick, a digital camera, a Web cam, a graphics tablet, and more. You typically plug the device into an expansion port on your computer. You can also expand or improve the capability of your computer by adding or upgrading expansion cards, such as sound cards, video cards, and so on.

Learning Objective 8:
Identify expansion ports and expansion cards, and explain how to use them

- **What is an expansion card?** An **expansion card** is a small circuit board that makes it possible for the computer to communicate with a peripheral device, such as a scanner, a joystick, or a digital camera. Expansion cards are also called expansion boards, controller cards, or adapters.

- **How are expansion cards connected to the computer?** An expansion card is plugged into an expansion slot on the motherboard. An **expansion slot** is a long, narrow socket on the motherboard into which you can plug an expansion card. Once an expansion card is plugged into the expansion slot, a peripheral device can be attached to the expansion card via the expansion port.

- **What is an expansion port?** An **expansion port** is a connector that passes data between a computer and a peripheral device. An expansion port is part of an expansion card. System units are designed with openings that make these ports accessible from outside the case. Common built-in expansion ports that come with a computer are shown in Figure B-27.
  - Graphics ports: connect display devices
  - FireWire ports: connect peripheral devices such as digital cameras and high-speed external data storage devices
  - Ethernet network ports: connect the computer to a wired network
  - eSATA ports: connect high-speed external data storage devices

- USB ports: connect peripheral devices such as mice, keyboards, flash drives, external drives, and cameras
- HDMI ports: connect high-definition video cables
- Audio ports: connect speakers, a headset, and/or a microphone

  In addition to the ones shown in the figure, you can add other expansion cards and ports.

- **Why would I want to add more expansion cards and ports?** You might want to add more cards and ports to upgrade existing expansion cards or to install new expansion cards to enhance sound or communications functionality. For example, you can install a high-end graphics card (sometimes called a video card) if you want to use the computer for advanced graphics or gaming.

- **How does an expansion card work?** The computer controls the peripheral device by sending data over circuits called a **data bus**. One part of the data bus runs between **RAM (Random Access Memory)** and the processor; the other part runs between RAM and various peripheral devices. RAM is volatile storage used by a computer. You will learn more about RAM later in this book. The segment of the data bus between RAM and the peripheral devices is called the **expansion bus**. As data moves along the expansion bus, it may travel through expansion slots, cards, ports, and cables. See Figure B-28 on the next page.

FIGURE B-27: Common expansion ports

FireWire port

Graphics ports

eSATA port

Ethernet network port

USB ports

Audio ports

Courtesy of MediaTechnics Corporation

FIGURE B-28: How the expansion bus works

| Processor | Local bus | RAM | Expansion bus | Expansion slots and expansion cards | Ports | Cable | Printer or other peripherals |

Expansion bus

Hard disk drive

● **How do I install an expansion card?** Usually, installing an expansion card requires you to open the system unit. Be sure to turn off the power to the system unit before opening a computer. An expansion card is inserted into an expansion slot in the motherboard. Expansion cards are built for only one type of slot. If you plan to add or upgrade a card in your computer, you must make sure the right type of slot is available on the motherboard. See Figure B-29.

FIGURE B-29: An expansion card slides into an expansion slot

● **Once I install the peripheral device or expansion card, will it work automatically?** PCs include a feature called Plug and Play. This means that once you plug a peripheral device into its port, the device is ready to use. Each peripheral device or expansion card requires software called a **device driver**. This software program sets up communication between your computer and the device or card. The directions supplied with your new peripheral device or card will include instructions on how to install the device driver if it does not happen automatically when you start the computer.

● **How do I connect most peripherals to my computer?** Today, many peripheral devices connect to your computer using an external **USB (universal serial bus) port**. USB is currently the most popular technology for connecting peripherals. A USB connector is shaped like a flat rectangle. Make sure you know which side of the plug is up; the top is usually labeled with the USB logo. See Figure B-30. USB ports are conveniently located on the front or sides of the system unit for easy access. Notebook computers often have USB ports on the sides and back of the computer case. Several types of storage devices, such as USB flash drives, also use USB connections.

FIGURE B-30: Plugging in a USB device

USB logo

● **Can I just unplug the peripheral device when I am done using it?** When you connect a peripheral device while the computer is operating, you are hot-plugging. You can only do this with USB and FireWire devices. Before you unplug a device, such as a USB flash drive, however, your computer might require notification. In Windows, you can give notification using the Safely Remove Hardware icon in the notification area of the taskbar. With a Mac, hold down the Control key, click the device icon, and then select Eject.

Talking Points: Why Recycle Computers?

For some people keeping up with technology means replacing their computer every few years. This raises the question: What should you do with your old, outdated computer? All of this electronic waste is creating e-garbage or technotrash—unwanted and outdated computers, monitors, printers, cell phones, PDAs, disk drives, disks, CDs, and DVDs. According to Greenpeace, 50 million tons of it is discarded every year. In the United States alone, almost eight printer cartridges are discarded every second. U.S. landfills already hold more than 2 million tons of computer parts, which contain toxic substances, such as lead, phosphorus, and mercury. For example, a computer monitor can contain up to six pounds of lead, and on average, contains four pounds of lead. People need to find creative ways to reuse their obsolete computers, such as retrofitting a hard drive to be a clock (see Figure B-31) or a monitor to be a fish tank.

" In this world of rapidly changing technology, disposal of computers and other electronic equipment has created a new and growing waste stream. "

Environmental Protection Agency (EPA) report.

Many computers end up in landfills because their owners are unaware of potential environmental hazards and simply toss them in the garbage. In addition, PC owners typically are not provided with information concerning the options for disposing of their old machines. Instead of throwing away your old computer, you might be able to sell it; donate it to a local school, church, or community program; have it hauled away by a professional recycling firm; or send it back to the manufacturer.

With the growing popularity of Internet auctions and dedicated computer reclamation sites, you might be able to get some cash for your old computer. At Web sites such as www.earth911.com, you can post an ad for your old computer equipment. Off the Web, you can find businesses that refurbish and sell old computers. Goodwill stores in many communities accept old computer equipment and arrange for it to be reused or recycled. Donating your old computer to a local organization does not actually eliminate the disposal problem, but it does delay it. Unfortunately, finding a new home for an old computer is not always easy. Most schools and community organizations have few resources for repairing broken equipment, so if your old computer is not in good working order, it could be more of a burden than a gift. In addition, your computer might be too old to be compatible with the other computers that are used in an organization.

FIGURE B-31: Creative use of old computer parts

Courtesy of TECOART LLC

It helps if you can donate software along with your old computer. To provide a legal transfer, include the software distribution media, manuals, and license agreement. And remember, once you donate the software, you cannot legally use it on your new computer unless it is freeware or shareware. If you cannot find an organization to accept your computer donation, look in your local Yellow Pages or on the Internet for an electronics recycling firm that will haul away your computer and recycle any usable materials.

In recent years, about half the states in the U.S. have taken some legislative action to curtail the rampant disposal of obsolete computer equipment. For example, Massachusetts has banned televisions and computer monitors from its landfills. In Maine it is illegal to dispose of computers or monitors—they have to be recycled in an environmentally sound way. But recycling can be costly—equipment needs to be collected, sorted, disassembled, and shipped to processing or disposal plants.

When Californians were faced with the prospect of tax hikes to deal with alarming increases in electronic waste, activists questioned if tax increases were fair to individual taxpayers who generate very little electronic waste. Now, consumers buying computers in California have to pay a recycling fee at the time of purchase. Maryland requires computer manufacturers to ante up an annual fee for electronic waste disposal.

Other lawmakers propose making manufacturers responsible for recycling costs and logistics. "Extended producer responsibility" refers to the idea of holding manufacturers responsible for the environmental effects of their products through their entire product life cycle, which includes taking them back, recycling them, or disposing of them. Some manufacturers currently participate in voluntary producer responsibility programs. Some companies have instituted PC recycling programs, which allow you to ship any make of computer, including system units, monitors, printers, and optional attachments, to a recycling center for a nominal fee. Consumers who buy toner cartridges for laser printers, such as from Hewlett-Packard, are provided with a postage-paid shipping box so they can return the cartridges for recycling. Dell offers free recycling for all Dell-branded products. Just connect to the Dell Web site, enter the equipment serial number, and fill out a shipping label.

The EPA advocates a national plan in which consumers, retailers, and manufacturers can cooperate to reduce electronic waste. Its Plug-in To eCycling Web site makes the point that "No national infrastructure exists for collecting, reusing, and recycling electronics." With laws that differ from state to state, consumers are often confused about how to dispose of their unwanted computers, monitors, CDs, and ink cartridges. These programs and others are important steps in the effort to keep our planet green.

As stated in an Environmental Protection Agency (EPA) report, "In this world of rapidly changing technology, disposal of computers and other electronic equipment has created a new and growing waste stream." Basic to the issue is the question of "Who pays?" Should it be the taxpayer, the individual, or the computer manufacturer?

> " U.S. landfills already hold more than 2 million tons of computer parts, which contain toxic substances, such as lead, phosphorus, and mercury. "

Expand the Ideas

1. Have you ever thrown away an old computer or other electronic device? If so, how did you dispose of it? Did you donate it, pass it along, or just throw it in the garbage? Write a short essay explaining what your options were at the time, any thoughts about recycling or donating you might have had, and exactly how you got rid of the old computer.

2. Research options for recycling electronic equipment in your local area. Create a chart showing ways to get rid of an old computer, and include the positive and negative aspects of each option. Include specific details for recycling or donating the computers, such as names and addresses.

3. Is it fair to ask consumers to pay a recycling tax on any electronic equipment that they purchase? Research the current trends. Include any important legislation or pending legislation in your area or around the world that you feel is relevant. Compile your findings in a short report. Include your opinion in the conclusion.

Key Terms & Unit Review

Key Terms

Access time
BD (Blu-ray Disc)
BD drive
Bit depth
Card reader
CD (compact disc)
CD drive
Color depth
CompactFlash (CF) card
Cursor
Data bus
Data transfer rate
Device driver
Direct access
Display device
Dot pitch
Dots per inch (dpi)
Drive bay
Duplex printer
Duty cycle

DVD (digital video disc or digital versatile disc)
DVD drive
Expansion bay
Expansion bus
Expansion card
Expansion port
Expansion slot
File
Graphics card
Hard drive
Ink-jet printer
Input device
Insertion point
Laser mouse
Laser printer
LCD (liquid crystal display)
Magnetic storage
Memory stick
Millisecond (ms)

Mouse
Network-enabled printer
OLED (organic light emitting diodes)
Optical mouse
Optical storage
Pages per minute (ppm)
Photo printer
Pixel (picture element)
Pointing device
Printer resolution
RAM (random access memory)
Random access
Recordable technology
Resolution
Response rate
Rewritable technology
Scanner
Screen size

SecureDigital (SD) card
Sequential access
Solid-state drive (SSD)
Solid-state storage
Solid-state technology
Storage capacity
Storage device
Storage medium
Storage technology
Tape cartridge
Tape storage
Toner
Touch screen technology
Touchpad
Trackball
Trackpad
USB flash drive
USB (universal serial bus) port
Viewing angle width

Unit Review

1. Make sure that you can use your own words to define the bold terms that appear throughout the unit.

2. Create a table to summarize what you know about different input devices discussed in this unit.

3. Create a table to summarize what you know about different printer technologies discussed in this unit.

4. Describe the advantages and disadvantages of magnetic storage, optical storage, and solid-state storage. Give an example of each type of storage. Summarize important uses for each type of storage technology.

5. List three facts that explain why a hard drive is the main storage device for a computer.

6. Describe the differences between the various CD, DVD, and BD technologies and why you would use one over the other.

7. Summarize the different technologies available for display devices. Be sure to include advantages and disadvantages.

8. List any peripheral devices that are attached to your computer. Describe what each one does. Be sure to identify each one as input, output, or storage. Identify how it is connected to your system unit.

9. If possible, identify USB ports on your computer and list any devices you have connected through USB ports. Are the ports on the front or back of the system unit?

10. Look at the front of your computer and identify the devices that are in the drive bays. List each device and explain what it does.

Concepts Review

Select the best answer.

1. A(n) _____ storage system uses lasers to read data.
   - a. magnetic
   - b. optical
   - c. solid state
   - d. tape

2. The _____ keys include the Home, End, and arrow keys.
   - a. main
   - b. numeric
   - c. navigation
   - d. function

3. A computer can move directly to any file on a(n) _____ access device.
   - a. random
   - b. optical
   - c. laser
   - d. sequential

4. A standard desktop computer uses a _____ as its primary pointing device.
   - a. navigation pad
   - b. track pad
   - c. keyboard
   - d. mouse

5. You should use a _____ , which has the most storage capacity, if you want to store a full-length feature movie.
   - a. USB drive
   - b. CD
   - c. DVD
   - d. Zip

6. Most DVD drives can read _____ and DVD formats.
   - a. Flash
   - b. Compact Flash
   - c. CD
   - d. BD

7. If you want to input data that currently exists in print format, you need to use a _____ .
   - a. microphone
   - b. scanner
   - c. digital camera
   - d. Web cam

8. A variety of compact storage cards and flash drives can be classified as _____ storage, which stores data in a nonvolatile, erasable, low-power chip.
   - a. solid-state
   - b. optical
   - c. magnetic
   - d. digital

9. The technologies used by mice to track motion are _____ and laser.
   - a. flash
   - b. random
   - c. optical
   - d. digital

10. A USB _____ drive is a portable storage device featuring a built-in connector that plugs directly into a computer's USB port and requires no card reader.
    - a. compact
    - b. Blu-ray
    - c. optical
    - d. flash

11. A _____ and a printer are the two main output devices for a computer system.
    - a. mouse
    - b. monitor
    - c. keyboard
    - d. storage device

12. _____ displays have a brighter image, better viewing angle, and faster response rate than standard LCD screens.
    - a. LED
    - b. DVD
    - c. CRT
    - d. PPM

13. People set the display settings for their monitor to a higher _____ to be able to see more on a screen.
    - a. dot pitch
    - b. resolution
    - c. viewing angle
    - d. access time

14. A(n) _____ is used to enter data in kiosks or on computers where a keyboard is not easily used.
    - a. BD
    - b. track pad
    - c. mouse
    - d. touch screen

15. If your computer and others are connected to a(n) _____ you can share a printer.
    - a. group
    - b. Internet
    - c. network
    - d. kiosk

16. Popular inexpensive printers for personal computers that produce quality color printouts are _____ printers.
    - a. ink jet
    - b. thermal
    - c. plasma
    - d. duplex

17. The front of the system case for a desktop computer contains several _____ where devices such as CD and BD/DVD drives are installed.
    - a. ports
    - b. expansion slots
    - c. drive bays
    - d. USB drives

18. An expansion _____, often located on the back of a desktop computer, is a connector that passes data between a computer and a peripheral device.
    - a. port
    - b. slot
    - c. drive
    - d. bay

19. Many peripheral devices connect to an external USB (universal serial _____) port.
    - a. belt
    - b. bed
    - c. bay
    - d. bus

20. A(n) _____ card is a small circuit board with a port that makes it possible for a computer to communicate with a peripheral device, such as a storage device.
    - a. expansion
    - b. add-on
    - c. peripheral
    - d. graphic

Independent Challenges

Independent Challenge 1

Storage technology has a fascinating history. Mankind has developed many ways to retain and store data. From the ancient days when Egyptians were writing on papyrus to modern day and futuristic technologies, societies have found ways to retain more and more information in permanent and safe ways.

For this Independent Challenge:

1. Research the history of storage technologies and create a timeline that shows the developments. Be sure to include such items as 78-rpm records, 8-track tapes, floppy disks (all formats including 8", 5.25", and 3.5"). Your research should yield some interesting technologies and systems. See Figure B-32 for some examples.

FIGURE B-32: Old storage media

© c./Shutterstock.com
© akva/Shutterstock.com
© Joseph McCullar/Shutterstock.com
© Patricia Hofmeester/Shutterstock.com
© JoLin/Shutterstock.com
© Péter Gudella/Shutterstock.com

2. For each technology, list the media, the device used to retrieve the information, two significant facts about the technology, the era in which it was used or was popular, and explain either what led to its demise or why it is still popular.

3. You can create the timeline using images or just words. This is a creative project. Your best research, artistic, and communication skills should come together to create this timeline.

Independent Challenge 2

It is important that you are familiar with the type of computer you use daily. If you do not own your own computer, use a typical computer in the lab at your school or use a friend's computer to complete this exercise. You may need to consult your technical resource person to help you complete this independent challenge.

For this Independent Challenge:

1. Identify the parts on your computer. What type of computer are you using? What kind of system unit do you have?

2. What display device is attached to the computer? What type of technology does it use? What is the screen size? Do you know the resolution?

3. Is there a printer attached to the computer? Is it a network printer? What type of printer is it (laser, ink-jet)? What is the brand, model?

4. What storage devices are part of the computer? Are there removable devices in use for the computer? What type are they? How big is the hard drive on the computer?

5. What peripheral devices are attached to your computer? List the name, manufacturer, and model number of each device, if available. How are these devices attached or connected to your system unit?

6. Draw a sketch of your computer. Label each component and identify what it does.

Independent Challenge 3

Technology is ever-changing so it can be impossible to predict all the ways you might use your computer in the future. But if you purchase a computer that is expandable, you will increase the possibility of using your computer for a long time.

For this Independent Challenge:

1. Refer to the ad in Figure B-33. Use one color marker to highlight all the components that come with this computer system that would make it possible for you to use this computer for video chatting, listening to music, and creating and editing photographs.

2. Refer again to the ad in Figure B-33. Use a second color marker to highlight all the parts of this system that are part of data storage systems.

3. Refer to the ad in Figure B-34. Review the system, the peripherals that come with it, and the possibilities for expansion. Use one color market to highlight all the components that can be used to expand the system with peripheral devices. Use another color to highlight the peripheral devices that come with the system.

4. Use the Internet to research three peripheral devices you would like to add to any computer system, then explain the following for each component:

   a. Why would you like to add this peripheral device?

   b. What is the cost to add this peripheral device?

   c. What technology would you use to attach this device to your computer?

FIGURE B-33: Computer ad for laptop PC

- Intel Core i5-520M processor 2.4 GHz 1066 MHz FSB
- 3 MB L2 cache
- 4 GB DDR3-800 MHz dual channel SDRAM
- 500 GB SATA HD (7200 rpm)
- 8x CD/DVD burner (Dual Layer DVD+/-R)
- 15.6" High Def (720p) LCD display screen
- 512 MB NVIDIA GeForce graphics card
- HD Audio 2.0 Support SRS Sound
- Integrated 1.3 megapixel Webcam
- 4 USB ports
- 1 IEEE 1394 port
- VGA and HDMI graphics ports
- 5-in-1 Media card reader
- Wireless networking 802.11 g/n
- Integrated 10/100 network card
- Windows 7 Home Premium 64-bit operating system
- Home/small business software bundle
- 1-year limited warranty

Courtesy of MediaTechnics Corporation; © Cengage Learning

FIGURE B-34: Computer ad for desktop PC

- Intel Core 2 Quad Q9650 processor 3.0 GHz, 1333 MHz FSB
- 12 MB L2 cache
- 4 GB DDR2-800 MHz dual channel SDRAM
- 500 GB SATA HD (7200 rpm)
- 16X max. DVD+/-R/RW SuperMulti drive
- 20" WUXGA monitor
- 512 MB NVIDIA GeForce graphics card
- Creative Sound Blaster X-Fi Xtreme Audio sound card
- Logitech speakers
- Mouse and keyboard
- Storage bay: Portable Media Drive Bay
- 6 USB ports: 2 front, 4 back
- 2 IEEE 1394
- 1 network port (RJ45 connector)
- 7 expansion slots
- Windows 7 operating system
- Home/small business software bundle
- Ink-jet printer
- 1-year limited warranty

Courtesy of MediaTechnics Corporation; Used with permission from Microsoft; © Cengage Learning

Guide to Buying a Computer

As you prepare to buy a computer, there are a lot of decisions you have to make. This book is designed to help you build the knowledge base you need to purchase a computer. In this unit, you were introduced to the basics of computer hardware. Each subsequent unit covers topics that can help you understand the type of computer you need, the software and services that will enhance your computing experience, such as Internet access, software purchases, and so forth. After each unit, you will be asked to answer questions by completing a worksheet. By the end of the book, your Guide to Buying a Computer worksheet will provide comprehensive information about buying a computer.

To help you organize the information you will need when you are ready to buy a computer, you should complete the following activities.

1. Storage devices are not the most expensive part of your buying decision. However, you should consider your options to make the best decisions for the data you want to store. Refer to the table below for an overview of storage technologies.

Storage device	Cost of device	Storage medium used with device	Capacity	Cost of media (Disk/Disc)	Technology	Is it portable?
Hard drive (Internal)			80 GB–2 TB		Magnetic	No
Hard drive (External)			80 GB–2 TB		Magnetic	Yes
CD-RW drive			700 MB		Optical	Yes
DVD+RW drive			8.5 GB		Optical	Yes
Blu-ray/DVD writer			50 GB		Optical	Yes
USB flash drive			512 MB–64 GB	N/A	Solid state	Yes
Solid-state drive (SSD) (Internal)			32 GB–256 GB	N/A	Solid state	No
Solid-state drive (SSD) (External)			32 GB–256 GB		Solid state	Yes

© Cengage Learning

2. Log on to the Internet and research each of the storage systems listed above. Use your research to complete the table.

3. Think of the way you might use storage. Select three of the storage devices listed above that meet your storage needs and explain why you chose them. Do you need only one of these three storage systems or do you need a combination?

_____

_____

_____

4. Deciding on the printer you want to buy depends on the tasks at hand. Are you planning to use the printer for a lot of reports? Are you printing photographs? Do you need speed? Log onto the Internet and research the two main printer types: inkjet and laser. Write the price comparisons for each.

_____

_____

_____

5. To continue what you started in Unit A, complete this portion of the Guide to Buying a Computer worksheet. Before beginning this part of the exercise, think about how you are planning to use the computer. You may be planning to use your computer for popular tasks such as email, browsing the Web, playing a few games, managing your checkbook, downloading digital music, and writing school papers. Another possibility is that you spend lots of time playing computer games. You might be purchasing the computer for someone who has special needs that must be considered.

As you continue to work through this book, you will learn more about personal computer systems. You will have the opportunity to answer more questions and complete other tables with information that will help you when it is time to buy a computer. To help you think about the hardware you need for a personal computer system, complete this portion of the Guide to Buying a Computer worksheet.

Guide to Buying a Computer: Hardware considerations

Questions to consider	Pages where the topic is covered in this book (refer to these pages to read more about the topic)	Notes (add additional comments, clarifications, or ideas about each topic)
What type of storage devices do you need permanently installed on the system unit?		
What size hard drive do you need?		
What types of removable storage do you need?		
Will you need to create or burn CDs? DVDs? BDs?		
What type of input devices do you need, such as a keyboard?		
What type of pointing devices will you need?		
Will you need to enter sound or voice data?		
Do you need a touch screen?		
What type of monitor do you want to buy? What are the main considerations that will help you make this decision?		
What type of printer do you want to buy?		
Do you need fast printing? Do you need to print in color? What are the main considerations that will help you make this decision?		
Do you need high-quality printouts? What are the main considerations that will help you make this decision?		
What peripheral devices will you need?		
If you choose a notebook, are these devices available?		
If you choose a desktop, is expansion possible?		
How many expansion slots should the computer system have?		
How many USB ports should the computer system have?		
If you choose a notebook or tablet computer, is expansion possible? How?		

Visual Workshop

The Talking Points section of this unit focused on the environmental impact of improperly discarded computers and other electronic devices. Some manufacturers are doing what they can to reduce the toxicity of components. Others are encouraging recycling. For this Visual Workshop, you will write a short paper about recycling computers based on information that you gather from the Internet. You will use the information you gather to create a poster for a campaign to promote Green Computing or responsible recycling in your community. Figure B-35 shows a possible theme for a poster.

1. Connect to the Internet and use your favorite search engine to search for and find Web pages to get an in-depth overview of the environmental impact and issues relating to the use and disposal of electronic devices and computers.

2. Determine the specific aspect of the issue that you will present in your paper. You might, for example, decide to focus on the toxic materials contained in computers that end up in landfills. You might investigate labor laws that protect those who dismantle computer parts for scrap. Current laws for shipping electronic devices such as monitors, printers, and computer parts to developing nations depend on the plan for the e-trash. If the plan is to use the computers, laws are more lenient. If the plan is to scrap the devices for their copper, lead, and gold, then the laws are more strict. Often people are hired to work in deplorable conditions without regard to the toxicity of the materials they are touching and breathing. You can investigate the government regulations that help to discourage the shipment of old computers across national borders or try to protect those who work in the scrapping industry.

3. Whatever aspect of the issue you decide to present, make sure that you can back up your discussion with facts and references to authoritative articles and Web pages. Place citations to your references (include the author's name, article title, date of publication, and URL) according to your instructor's directions, such as at the end of your paper as endnotes, on each page as footnotes, or in parentheses following the appropriate paragraphs. Follow your instructor's directions for submitting your paper via email or as a printed document.

4. After completing the paper, consider the main points that you want to convey in a poster to your community. Use paper to sketch out your ideas. Complete the poster using poster board. Follow your instructor's directions for submitting the poster.

FIGURE B-35: Recycling poster

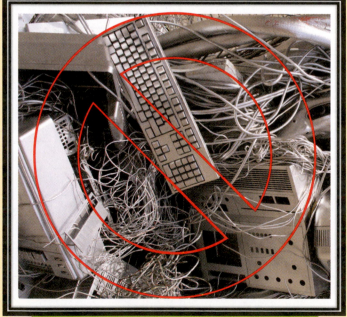

© Shipov Oleg/Shutterstock.com; © Cengage Learning

UNIT C Concepts

Computer Software

Learning Objectives

1. List and describe computer software categories
2. Explain copyright law and define the different software licenses
3. Explain how to install and uninstall software
4. Identify the basic functions and features of operating systems
5. Compare operating systems
6. Describe utility software, including device drivers
7. Define office productivity software, and name examples in each major category
8. Define graphics software, and name examples in each major category
9. Name other categories of application software, and give examples in each major category

Courtesy of Emily Bunin

LESSON TOPICS

- Computer Software
- Licenses and Copyrights
- How to Install and Uninstall Software
- Operating Systems—An Overview
- Operating Systems—A Comparison
- Utility Software
- Office Productivity Software
- Graphics Software
- Other Application Software

Talking Points: What is the Downside to Software Piracy?

Computer Software

Software, also called **computer programs**, gives computers the instructions and data necessary to carry out tasks. Software is used to create documents or graphics. Software is used to help schedule classes or to listen to music. Software makes it possible to communicate using computers. Most software uses a **graphical user interface (GUI)**. This allows you to give the computer commands using pointing devices and graphics such as menus, buttons, icons, links, and more.

Learning Objective 1:
List and describe computer software categories

- **When do I use software?** You use software every time you use your desktop, notebook, or tablet computer. In addition, you use software when you use your mobile phone, digital camera, retail and banking machines, some home appliances, cars, some medical devices, and much more. Software carries out your commands anytime you press buttons or touch a screen to tell a machine what to do.

- **Are there different types of software?** Yes. Software is usually categorized as either system software or application software. **System software** is used by the computer for tasks that help the computer work. For example, you use system software to run your computer and all the programs on it. It can diagnose a problem with your hard drive, printer, or Internet connection. **Application software** helps you carry out tasks such as sending an email, getting you street-by-street driving directions, editing a photo, or writing a report.

Software can be grouped in subcategories according to how the software is used. System software can be grouped into subcategories for operating systems, utilities, and device drivers. Application software can be grouped according to tasks, such as producing documents, creating spreadsheets, or communicating with others. Figure C-1 shows common ways to categorize system software and application software. Some software can be in more than one category, so use these categories as a general guideline.

- **Are there other ways to group software?** Yes. Software applications can also be categorized according to their accessibility and where they are installed. These categories include local applications, Web applications, portable applications, or mobile applications.

FIGURE C-1: Examples of software categories

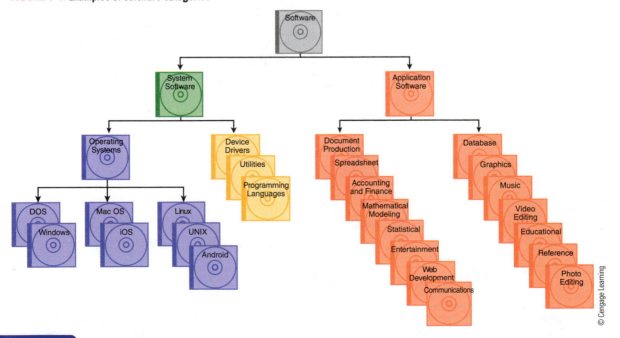

© Cengage Learning

- **What is a local application?** A **local application** is software that is installed on a computer. When you install a local application, the program files are placed in the appropriate folders on the computer's hard drive. After the software is installed, the computer makes sure the program is ready to run.

- **What is a Web application?** A **Web application** (also called **Web app** or **cloudware**) is software that is accessed with a Web browser. Instead of running locally on a computer, much of the program code for the software runs on a remote computer connected to the Internet or other computer network. Web apps are available for many of the same applications that run locally. These include email, calendars, databases, photo sharing, project management, maps, games, and even word processing. Web apps make it possible for groups of people to collaborate on projects in multiple locations.

  The advantage of a Web app is that you can use it anywhere you have access to a computer connected to the Web. However, there are also disadvantages when using Web apps. For example, you don't have access to the Web app if you lose power to your computer or if you lose your Internet connection. And, you don't have access if the Internet server hosting the Web app goes down.

- **What is a portable application?** A **portable application** is designed to run from a removable storage device, such as a USB flash drive. Program files are not installed on the hard drive, and no configuration data is stored on the computer. When the media containing the portable software is removed from the computer, no trace of the portable application is left on the computer. Portable software can only be used when the removable storage device is connected to a computer.

- **What is a mobile application?** A **mobile application** (or **app**) is designed to run on mobile devices such as smartphones and tablet computers. Mobile apps include games, calendars, stock market trackers, tour guides, highway traffic monitors, news feeds, and more.

- **How do I know if a software program will work on my computer?** The **system requirements**, which specify the operating system and minimum hardware capacities, give you the information you need to know if a software program will work on a computer. You can find the system requirements on the software manufacturer's Web site or on the software packaging. See Figure C-2.

FIGURE C-2: System requirements

System Requirements

Operating Systems: Windows 7/Vista/XP
Processor: Intel Pentium or Core or equivalent
Memory: 1 GB or more
Hard Drive Space: 10 MB for installation
Network Protocol: TCP/IP
Network Connection: 10/100 Ethernet LAN/WAN, cable modem, DSL router, ISDN router, or dial-up modem

eCourse Internet Works

2012 eCourseWare Corp. All rights reserved. eCourse is a registered trademark of eCourseWare Corp.

© Courtesy of MediaTechnics Corporation

Installed software that comes with new personal computers

Most computers are sold with the operating system installed so you can turn on the machine and use it right away. The operating system, Windows 7 for example, typically includes a Web browser, media player, and several simple programs. These include a simple text editor, a few games, and some gadgets. Some computers come with application software that you can use to create documents, manage budgets, and produce presentations. Your computer may come with antivirus software. Be sure to check the terms of the application software that is installed. The trend today is for manufacturers to install trial software that you can use free for a few months. To continue using the software beyond the trial period, however, you have to pay for it. If you're purchasing a computer to do a task that requires specialized software, you should factor its cost into the cost of your computer system. Check the specifications listed on the software box to make sure your new computer has enough memory and processing speed to run it.

UNIT C — Concepts

Licenses and Copyrights

Just because it is easy to copy and share other people's documents, photographs, and music though email or post it on your Web site, doesn't mean it's legal to do so. Copyright and intellectual property laws, as well as the software license, govern how you can use **digital content.** This includes digital content you buy at a brick-and-mortar store or download from the Web using a computer. Understanding copyright law and software licenses for digital content will help you avoid legal troubles.

Learning Objective 2:
Explain copyright law and define the different software licenses

● **What is copyright? Copyright** is a legal protection that grants the author of an original work an exclusive right to copy, distribute, sell, and modify that work, except under special circumstances described by copyright laws. Exceptions include the purchaser's right to copy software from a distribution disc or Web site to a computer's hard drive in order to install it.

● **If I don't see the © symbol, does it mean the software is not protected?** Most software displays a **copyright notice**, such as "© 2014 Microsoft Corporation. All Rights reserved," on one of its starting screens. However, this notice is not required by law. As a result, even programs without a copyright notice are protected by copyright law. People who go around copyright law and illegally copy, distribute, or modify software are sometimes called **software pirates.** Their illegal copies are referred to as **pirated software.**

● **What is a software license?** A **software license**, or **license agreement**, is a legal contract that lets you know the ways in which you may use or share that computer program. Once you purchase software, or even if you get software for free, you can only use the software as defined by the software license. The type of license determines how the software is classified legally.

● **How is software classified legally?** Software is legally classified in two categories: public domain and proprietary. **Public domain software** is not protected by copyright because the copyright has expired, or the author has placed the program in the public domain making it available without restriction. Public domain software may be freely copied, distributed, and even resold. The primary restriction on public domain software is that you are not allowed to apply for a copyright on it.

Creative commons is an organization committed to freely sharing content on the Internet. See Figure C-3. Their Web site explains licensing options for distributing software.

FIGURE C-3: Creative commons Web site

www.creativecommons.org

Proprietary software has restrictions on its use that are delineated by copyright, patents, or license agreements. Some proprietary software is distributed commercially, whereas some of it is free. Depending on the licensing rights, proprietary software is distributed as commercial software, demoware, shareware, freeware, or open source software. These classifications determine the software license.

● **What is commercial software? Commercial software** is typically sold in stores or on Web sites. Although you buy this software, you actually purchase only the right to use it under the terms of the software license. Some commercial software is available as a trial version, called **demoware.** Demoware is distributed free and often comes preinstalled on new computers. Demoware is limited in some way until you pay for it. Demoware publishers usually take steps to prevent users from overriding time limitations.

● **What is shareware?** **Shareware** is copyrighted software marketed under a try-before-you-buy policy. It typically includes a license that permits you to use the software for a trial period. To use it beyond the trial period, you must send in a registration fee. A shareware license usually allows you to make copies of the software and distribute it to others. If they choose to use the software, they must send in a registration fee. Registration fee payment relies on the honor system. Unfortunately, many shareware authors collect only a fraction of the money they deserve for their programming efforts.

● **What is freeware?** **Freeware** is copyrighted software that is available without a fee. Because the software is protected by copyright, you cannot do anything with it that is not expressly allowed by copyright law or by the author. Typically, the license for freeware permits you to use the software, copy it, and give it away, but does not permit you to alter it or sell it. Many utility programs, device drivers, and some games are available as freeware.

● **What is open source software?** **Open source software** makes the program instructions available to programmers who want to modify and improve the software. Open source software may be sold or distributed free of charge, but it must, in every case, include the source code. The Firefox browser is open source software. The Open Source Initiative is a non-profit corporation that advocates for open source software. See Figure C-4.

FIGURE C-4: Open Source Initiative

The OSI logo trademark is the trademark of Open Source Initiative.

● **Do I have to accept the license agreement to run the software?** Yes, usually before you install and run a program, you have to agree to the terms as stated in the EULA (end-user license agreement). The EULA displays on the screen when you install the software. You can indicate that you accept the terms by clicking a designated button or check box labeled OK, I agree, or I accept. See Figure C-5.

FIGURE C-5: Microsoft Office 2010 software license

Used with permission from Microsoft

● **Since I didn't actually sign anything, am I still legally bound to this license?** Yes, while most legal contracts require signatures before the terms take effect, software publishers typically use two techniques to validate a software license. A **shrink-wrap license** goes into effect as soon as you open the packaging. Downloaded software has an **installation agreement** that goes into effect as soon as you click the option to accept the terms of the agreement.

● **What software licenses are available?** A **single-user license** limits use of the software to one person at a time. A **site license** is generally priced at a flat rate and allows software to be used on all computers at a specific location. A **multiple-user license** is priced per user and allows the allocated number of people to use the software at any time. A **concurrent-use license** is priced per copy and allows a specific number of copies to be used at the same time.

How does digital technology affect intellectual property laws?

Intellectual property refers to the ownership of certain types of information, ideas, or representations. It includes patents, trademarks, and copyrighted material, such as music, photos, software, books, and films. In the past, such works were difficult and expensive to copy. However, digital technology has made it easy to produce copies with no loss in quality from the original. Pirating software is simple and inexpensive. It has caused significant revenue loss for software publishers, as well as recording studios, and film producers. The fight against piracy takes many forms. Governments have passed strict anti-piracy laws. Technology is available that scrambles and encrypts content. Several companies use digital rights management technology that physically prevents copying. Organizations such as the Software & Information Industry Association have committed to consumer education and created anti-piracy videos that are shown to the public. See Figure C-6.

FIGURE C-6: Educating the public

Courtesy of the Software & Information Industry Association

How To Install and Uninstall Software

You often want to add application software or apps to your digital device. Software can be obtained in many ways, such as on distribution media (CD, DVD, or BD) or downloaded from the Web. Unless you are using Web apps, you must install software before you can use it. Installation procedures depend on your computer's operating system and whether the software is a local, portable, or mobile application. In addition to installing software, you should also know how to upgrade your software and how to uninstall software you no longer need.

Learning Objective 3:
Explain how to install and uninstall software

● **What does it mean to install software?** When you install software, you are copying the software from a distribution media, such as from a CD, DVD, BD or the Web, to your hard drive so you can use the program. You generally won't install the OS. It usually comes installed on the computer or mobile device when you buy it.

● **How do I start the installation process?** To install software from a CD or a DVD, place the disc in the CD or DVD drive. Once the disc is in the drive, you will see blinking lights on the drive and information will appear on your screen as a setup program starts.

To install software from the Web, read any information on the Web site about installing the software, then click the download link. See Figure C-7. The files you need will be downloaded and copied to a folder on your computer. Downloaded software files are usually zipped into one large compressed file. Compressed files are smaller so they download faster. Some compressed files are zip files, others are executable files. You will learn about file compression in the lesson on utilities. Once the files are downloaded, a setup program starts.

FIGURE C-7: **Downloading software**

If you are downloading from a trusted site and have antivirus software running, click the Run button in the File Download dialog box.

The files are downloaded to your computer.

● **What is a setup program?** A **setup program** is a series of steps designed to guide you through the installation process. You follow directions as prompted on the screen to complete the installation process. If you are installing software from the Web, the downloaded zip file is unzipped into the original collection of files and into a folder that you can specify during the installation process. As part of the installation process, you will be asked to accept the end user license agreement (EULA).

● **How do I know where the software is installed?** During the installation process, you will be prompted to specify the location where you want to store the program files. See Figure C-8. You can use the default folder specified by the setup program or a folder of your own choosing. You can also create a new folder during the setup process. Generally, when you install software, the new software files are placed in the appropriate folders on your computer's hard drive.

FIGURE C-8: **Select the location on the hard drive for the files**

● **What type of installation should I choose?** During the installation process, you are asked what type of installation you want: full or custom. If you select a full installation, the setup program copies all files and data from the distribution medium to the hard drive of your computer system. A full installation gives you access to all features of the software. If you select a custom installation, the setup program displays a list of software features for your selection.

After you select the features you want, the setup program copies only the selected program and data files to your hard drive. A custom installation can save space on your hard drive but limits functionality of the program because not all features are installed. Select the installation option that best meets your needs. See Figure C-9.

FIGURE C-9: Select the type of installation

⦿ **Full Installation**
○ **Custom Installation**

© Cengage Learning

● **What else happens during the installation process?** As part of the installation process, your computer performs any software or hardware configurations necessary to make sure the program is ready to run.

● **How do I start the program?** When the installation is complete, you should start the program you just installed to make sure it works. Techniques for running applications depend on your computer's operating system. On most personal computers, you can double-click an application desktop icon, click a program icon on the taskbar or Dock, or you can select the application from a menu. See Figure C-10.

FIGURE C-10: Many ways to start an application

Double-click a desktop icon

Click the Start button, then click a menu item

Click a program button on the taskbar

Used with permission from Microsoft

● **Do I have to activate the software?** Yes. Although you may be allowed to run a program for a set number of times before activation, generally you need to activate the program for long-term use. To combat piracy, many software publishers require users to type in a validation code to complete an installation and activate the software. A **validation code** is a long sequence of numbers and letters that is typically supplied separately from the software itself. Validation codes can usually be found on distribution media packaging. If you download the software, the validation code is sent to you via email.

● **What is software registration?** Software registration collects your personal information, such as your email address. Generally, product activation is not the same as registration. A few software publishers tie activation and registration together. Activation is required but registration is voluntary.

● **Why would I want to register my software?** You register your software in order to receive product information and updates.

● **What are software updates?** After you install your software, several types of updates are usually available. These updates are patches, service packs, and software upgrades. **Patches** are small programs designed to correct, secure, or enhance an existing program. **Service packs** are a collection of updates, fixes, and/or enhancements to a software program delivered in the form of a single installable package. They are usually distributed over the Internet. Patches and service packs automatically install themselves when you download them. **Software upgrades** are available to consumers who already have a software program installed. Software upgrades are usually less expensive than buying the software package new.

● **How do I remove software I don't need anymore?** Most software programs come with an uninstall program. In addition, most operating systems, such as Windows and Mac OS, provide access to an uninstall program. Uninstall programs are designed to delete all the related program files from your computer's program and system folders on the hard drive and from the desktop.

Installing portable software

Portable software is so simple to install that it is sometimes referred to as install-free software. Installation is simply a matter of transferring program files to the media on which they are supposed to run. For example, suppose that you want to run OpenOffice Portable from a USB flash drive. You can download the OpenOffice Portable zip file and then simply unzip it so that the files are saved on the USB flash drive. Other examples of portable applications include Thunderbird (email), Firefox (browser), and FileZilla (ftp upload and download). Each of these portable applications is designed to run from USB flash drives.

Operating Systems— An Overview

An **operating system (OS)** is system software. It is the master controller for all of the activities that take place in any computer system, including desktop, notebook, and tablet computers as well as smartphones and other mobile devices. The operating system determines how people interact with a digital device. It also controls how a digital device communicates with other computers on a network or peripheral devices such as printers and scanners.

Learning Objective 4:
Identify the basic functions and features of an operating system

● **How do I start the operating system?** The operating system starts each time you turn on your computer or digital device. The first task of the operating system when you turn on a computer is to start the **boot process**. This is why turning on a computer is also called "booting a computer." Six major events happen during the boot process. Refer to Table C-1.

TABLE C-1: Six steps in the boot process

Step	Description
1. Power up	When you turn on the power switch, the power light is illuminated and power is distributed to the computer circuitry.
2. Start bootstrap program	The processor begins to execute the bootstrap program that is stored in permanent memory called ROM.
3. Power-on self-test (POST)	The operating system performs diagnostic tests of several crucial system parts.
4. Identify peripheral devices	The operating system identifies the peripheral devices that are connected to the computer and checks their settings.
5. Load operating system	The operating system is copied from the hard drive to Random Access Memory (RAM).
6. Check configuration and customization	The operating system reads configuration data and the processor executes any customized startup routines.

© Cengage Learning

● **What does the operating system do?** Your computer's operating system ensures that input and output proceed in an orderly manner. It provides buffers to hold data while the computer is busy with other tasks. A **buffer** is an area of memory that holds data from one device while it is waiting to be transferred to another device. By using a keyboard buffer, for example, your computer never misses one of your keystrokes, regardless of how fast you type. In addition, the operating system manages a computer's resources by interacting with your computer's software and hardware. See Figure C-11.

FIGURE C-11: Example of how the operating system works

1. You issue the Print command while using application software, such as a word processor.

2. The word processing application signals the operating system that a document must be sent to the printer.

Printer Driver

3. The operating system communicates the document data to the device driver for the printer.

4. The device driver controls the printer as it prints the document.

Courtesy of MediaTechnics Corporation

● **What is a computer's resource?** The term **resource** refers to any computer component that is required to perform work. For example, computer resources include the CPU (central processing unit), RAM, storage devices, and peripherals. While you interact with application software, your computer's operating system is busy behind the scenes with resource management tasks such as those listed in Figure C-12.

FIGURE C-12: Resource management tasks

Manage processor resources to handle simultaneous input, output, and processing tasks

Manage memory by allocating space for all the programs and data that are in use during a computing session

Keep track of storage resources so that files and programs can be found

Ensure that input and output proceed in an orderly manner by communicating with peripheral devices

Establish basic elements of the user interface such as the appearance of the desktop, menus, and toolbars

Courtesy of MediaTechnics Corporation; © Sergei Devyatkin/Shutterstock.com; Used with permission from Microsoft

● **How does the operating system let you know there is a problem?** The operating system displays messages on the device screen if it encounters a problem. For example, if a device driver or a peripheral device is not performing correctly, the operating system usually displays an on-screen warning about the problem so you can take corrective action.

● **How do I know what programs are currently running on my computer?** When using Windows, you can open the Task Manager to see a list of programs. See Figure C-13. The operating system is **multitasking** when more than one program is running at one time. In addition to programs, many activities—called processes—compete for the attention of your computer's processor. Most processes are programs that run in the background to carry out tasks for the operating system, device drivers, and applications. You can see the list of processes that are running by clicking the Processes tab in the Task Manager.

FIGURE C-13: Windows 7 Task Manager

Used with permission from Microsoft

● **How do I use the operating system?** Although its main purpose is to control what happens behind the scenes of a computer system, many operating systems provide tools to make computing easier or more fun for you. You can use these operating system utilities to control and customize your computer equipment and work environment. The Windows Control Panel lets you personalize many features. See Figure C-14. For example, using options in the Control Panel, you can change your display properties, such as adjusting your screen resolution or setting a screen saver. Table C-2 lists some ways you interact with your computer's OS.

FIGURE C-14: Windows 7 Control Panel

Used with permission from Microsoft

TABLE C-2: Ways you use an operating system

You can	Most operating systems
Launch programs	display graphical objects such as icons, a Start button, and the Programs menu that you can use to start programs
Manage files	include programs, such as Windows Explorer, that allow you to view a list of folders and files, move them to different storage devices, copy them, rename them, and delete them
Get help	offer a Help system that you can use to find out more about the OS, such as how various commands work
Customize the user interface environment	provide utilities that help you customize your screen display, system sounds, security and access
Configure equipment and install and uninstall programs	provide access to utilities that help you set up and configure your computer's hardware and peripheral devices, install and uninstall software

© Cengage Learning

Operating Systems— A Comparison

When you purchase a personal computer, it generally comes with the OS already installed. When you purchase a mobile device, it also usually comes with an operating system already installed. The operating system you use depends on the type of personal computer or digital device you use, as well as the type of processor running your personal computer or digital device. The operating system determines the user interface on your digital device.

Learning Objective 5:
Compare operating systems

● **What is a user interface?** A **user interface** is the combination of hardware and software that helps you communicate with a computer. Your computer's user interface includes a display device, mouse, and keyboard as well as software elements, such as icons, toolbars, menus, and command buttons. This combination of hardware and software determines how you interact with your computer. When a user interface has graphical elements, it is called a graphical user interface (GUI).

● **What are the main operating systems in use today for personal computers?** The three main operating systems for personal computers in use today are **Windows**, **Mac OS**, and **Linux**. The Windows operating system is installed on PCs. The Mac OS is installed on Apple computers. Linux can be installed on PCs. Each operating system has different versions, such as home or professional.

● **Why are there different versions of an operating system?** There are different versions to meet the wide range of consumer needs. For example, your home personal computer probably doesn't need as powerful an operating system as a computer used in a large business. You need your computer to perform basic tasks. A business may need its computers to perform basic tasks as well as network with other computers in the company. Different versions allow users to buy the operating system to best meet their needs. For example, Microsoft offers several versions, called editions, of the Windows operating system for various markets. As a consumer, you can choose from among these editions of Windows 7: Home Premium, Professional, and Ultimate. Each edition has features that meet specific markets or needs.

In addition to the desktop version, there are also server and embedded versions of Microsoft Windows. Server editions are designed for LAN, Internet, and Web servers. Embedded editions are designed for handheld devices, such as tablets and mobile phones.

● **Which version of Windows will probably be on my computer?** If you purchase a PC, it will probably be running the most current desktop version of Windows for personal computers. Windows 7 is a desktop operating system. See Figure C-15. Since its introduction in 1985, Windows has evolved through several versions. The latest version boasts easy personalization, enhanced security, flexible file management, and powerful search capabilities. A newer version, Windows 8, is currently being released. The Start button on the taskbar helps you recognize that the computer is running Windows.

FIGURE C-15: Windows 7 User Interface

Used with permission from Microsoft

● **What operating system is available for the Macintosh computer?** Mac OS X (the X can be pronounced either as ten or the letter X) is the operating system used on Apple Macintosh computers. Like Windows, Mac OS X has also been through a number of versions.

Versions of Mac OS X are named after big cats; the current version is named Lion. Previous versions include Snow Leopard, Cheetah, Puma, Jaguar, Panther, Tiger, and Leopard. The Apple logo at the top of the screen on the menu bar and the Dock at the bottom of the desktop help you recognize that the computer is running Mac OS.

● **What is Linux?** Linux is an operating system that is available as a free download. Linux was developed by Linus Torvalds in 1991. The Linux operating system is distributed under the terms of a **General Public License (GPL),** which allows everyone to make copies for his or her own use, to give it to others, or to sell it. This licensing policy has encouraged programmers to develop Linux utilities, software, and enhancements. Linux is gaining popularity as a personal computer operating system. See Figure C-16.

FIGURE C-16: The Ubuntu Linux operating system interface

Courtesy of Canonical Ltd.

● **What operating systems run on tablet computers?** Leading tablet operating systems include Windows, BlackBerry®, Android, and iOS. Tablets running Windows include Lenovo, IdeaPad, and HP Slate. Tablets running the BlackBerry® Tablet OS include the BlackBerry®

PlayBook™ tablet. Tablets running Android are made by many manufacturers including Motorola, Samsung, and Toshiba. Apple tablets run the proprietary iOS Apple operating systems. See Figure C-17.

FIGURE C-17: Tablet computer operating systems

BlackBerry®, RIM®, Research In Motion® and related trademarks, names and logos are the property of Research In Motion Limited and are registered and/or used in the U.S. and countries around the world.; Used under license from Research In Motion Limited.; © Christine Glade/iStockphoto

● **What operating systems run on smartphones?** Smartphones are essentially communications devices so their operating systems need to accommodate voice as well as data on very small screens. These special requirements are met by several operating systems. Some manufactures produce smartphone models that use different mobile operating systems. See Figure C-18. For example, you can buy one Sony smartphone that runs Android and a different Sony smartphone that runs Windows Mobile 7.

FIGURE C-18: Smartphone operating systems

From left: Used by permission from Microsoft; Courtesy of Google Inc. Android is a trademark of Google Inc.; © amriphoto/iStockphoto

Comparing types of operating systems

Operating systems for computers, notebooks, and mobile devices provide many similar services, such as scheduling processor resources, managing memory, loading programs, managing input and output, and creating the user interface. But because mobile devices, such as smartphones and tablets, tend to be used for less sophisticated tasks, their operating systems are simpler and significantly smaller. By keeping the operating system small, it can be stored in ROM. Because operating systems for these mobile devices do not need to load the OS from the disk into RAM, these mobile devices are ready almost instantly when they are turned on.

Operating systems for mobile devices often provide built-in support for touch screens, handwriting input, wireless networking, and cellular communications. Touch screen input makes it possible to use fingers to swipe, squeeze, and expand content in order to control the size and placement of objects on the screen.

Utility Software

As you use your computer, you will find it is important to keep it in good working order. Utility software can help you do just that. **Utility software** (also referred to as **utilities**) is a type of system software designed to perform a specialized task. Examples of utility software include diagnostic and maintenance tools, setup wizards, communications programs, security software, device drives, and gadgets.

Learning Objective 6:
Describe utility software, including device drivers

● **Why do I need utility software?** You need utility software to help maintain your computer and safeguard your files. Utility software helps you monitor and configure settings for your computer system hardware, the operating system, and application software. Utilities are used for backing up, securing, permanently deleting, and cleaning up files on hard drives. These utilities include security features for shredding files so they cannot be recovered. Other utilities can help you recover files deleted (but not shredded) by mistake. Utility software includes diagnostics that track down file errors and other problems that prevent computers from running at peak efficiency. These utilities can also give your PC a performance-enhancing tune-up. See Figure C-19.

FIGURE C-19: Example of a utility to optimize your system

Courtesy of Systweak

● **Do any utilities come with the operating system?** Yes. A variety of utilities are included with your operating system. For example, Figure C-20 shows the System and Security utilities, which provides access to the many Windows operating system utilities. You use the Control Panel to access the System and Security utilities. You can access the Control Panel using the Windows Start menu.

FIGURE C-20: Microsoft Windows System and Security utilities

Used with permission from Microsoft

● **Do I always have to run the utilities or are some automatic?** There are operating system utilities that run in the background. For example, one Windows utility periodically sets a **restore point**, which is a snapshot of your computer settings. Restore points are created automatically every week, and just before significant system events, such as the installation of a program or device driver. If a hard drive problem causes system instability, you might be able to roll back your system to a restore point when your computer was operational. You can manually set restore points, too. For example, you might want to set a restore point before setting up a network. You do this so you can restore your system to the way it was before the installation if unexpected problems are created when you set up a network. This can save you a lot of time and aggravation.

● **Do I have to use the utilities that come with my operating system or do I have other choices?** You have choices. In addition to utilities that come with your operating system, other third-party utilities are available. You will typically use utilities from third-party vendors because operating system utilities are often not as comprehensive or do not provide as many features as third-party utilities. Third-party utilities are designed by companies that specialize in system maintenance or security.

● **What are some utility programs I should know about?** If you work with large files, you might use a **compression utility** to reduce file size for quick transmission or efficient storage. The Windows operating system comes with a file compression utility. Many computer owners prefer to use a third-party utility, such as WinZip, IZArc, Quick Zip, or PKZIP.

You will also want to use **security utilities**. These utilities can scan incoming and outgoing files to be sure they are safe. They can scan your applications to see if any are missing security patches. They can also help you control nuisance ads, intrusion attempts, and spam. Other security-related utilities include file-encryption software that scrambles file content for storage or transmission. You can also buy utilities that remove Internet history lists, files, and graphics from disk storage locations that can be scattered in many parts of the hard drive.

● **Can utilities help me customize my desktop?** Yes, for example, you can use utilities to customize your desktop with screen savers that display clever graphics when the machine is idle. Different themes can change the way fonts are displayed in menus and icons in programs. Themes can also customize sounds that are played when operating system events occur. For example, when an action doesn't work, you might hear a buzzer.

● **What is PDF?** PDF stands for Portable Document File. The PDF file format is used so that a document can be read by people regardless of what type of computers they are using or the software they have installed on their computers. To read a PDF file, you need a document reader utility, such as the popular and free Adobe Reader. Links to download Adobe Reader are available on many Web sites. See Figure C-21.

FIGURE C-21: Adobe Reader is a free utility to read PDF files

● **What is a device driver?** A **device driver** is a type of utility software that helps a peripheral device to establish communication with a computer. Device drivers are used by printers, monitors, graphics cards, sound cards, network cards, modems, storage devices, mice, and scanners. Once installed, a device driver starts automatically when it is needed. Device drivers usually run in the background, without opening a window on the screen. On a PC, the Windows Device Manager offers access to device drivers so you can check if they are working, change settings, and check the device driver's version number to compare it with the most recent version posted online. See Figure C-22.

FIGURE C-22: Checking device driver details

● **What is a desktop gadget or widget?** A **desktop gadget** or **gadget** (called a **widget** on Apple computers) is a utility program that is placed on a computer's desktop. It looks like a control and might display a snippet of information. Some examples of desktop gadget include clocks, calendars, calculators, news aggregators, sticky notes, and weather stations. Gadgets usually start automatically when a computer boots, and they remain on the desktop until the computer is shut down. Figure C-23 illustrates some popular gadgets on a PC desktop.

FIGURE C-23: Desktop gadgets

Computer Software

Office Productivity Software

If you work in an office, you will use a computer to create documents, schedule meetings, send email, manage numbers, make presentations, and organize data. **Office productivity software** (also called **productivity software**) is generally defined as the software that allows you to be productive in an office setting. It integrates these major software categories: word processing, spreadsheet, presentation, database, and scheduling.

Learning Objective 7:
Define office productivity software, and name examples in each major category

● **What is word processing software? Word processing software** is used to produce documents, such as reports, letters, books, blogs, and manuscripts. If you are writing a paper, writing a blog, or organizing your résumé, you will probably use a word processor. Word processors allow you to apply a theme and styles to create a unified look across documents using the same word processing program. They give you the ability to create, check the spelling, edit, and format a document on the screen before you commit it to paper. See Figure C-24. Microsoft Word and OpenOffice Writer are examples of word processors.

● **What is spreadsheet software? Spreadsheet software** is ideal for projects that require repetitive calculations, such as budgeting, maintaining a grade book, balancing a checkbook, tracking investments, and calculating loan payments. Because it is so easy to experiment with different numbers, spreadsheet software is useful for what-if analysis. Spreadsheet software can generate colorful graphs and charts based on the data in the spreadsheet. Spreadsheet software provides the tools to create electronic worksheets. A **worksheet** is a grid of columns and rows. See Figure C-25. Microsoft Excel and OpenOffice Calc are examples of spreadsheet programs.

FIGURE C-24: Checking the spelling of a document in Microsoft Word

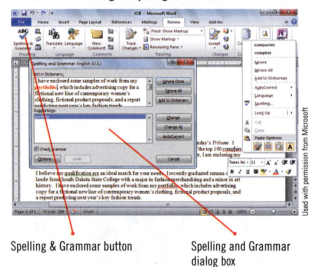

Spelling & Grammar button

Spelling and Grammar dialog box

Used with permission from Microsoft

FIGURE C-25: A spreadsheet in OpenOffice Calc

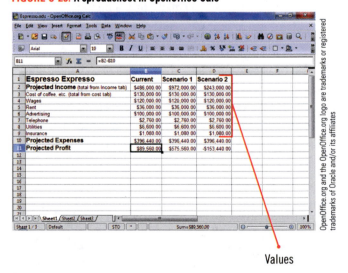

Values

OpenOffice.org and the OpenOffice.org logo are trademarks or registered trademarks of Oracle and/or its affiliates

Software suites

A **software suite** is a collection of application software sold as a single package. See Figure C-26. Purchasing a software suite is usually much less expensive than purchasing each application in the suite separately. Because all the applications in a suite are produced by the same software publisher, they tend to have similar user interfaces and provide an easy way to transport data from one application to another. The disadvantage of a software suite is that it might include applications you do not need. You should calculate the price of the applications you do need and compare that to the cost of the suite.

FIGURE C-26: A software suite

Used with permission from Microsoft

● **What is database software?** **Database software** provides the tools needed to create a database. A **database** is a collection of data that is stored electronically as a series of records in tables. See Figure C-27. Database software can help you print reports, export data to other programs (such as to a spreadsheet, where you can graph the data), and transmit data to other computers. A database can contain any sort of data, such as your music collection, a university's student records, or a company's customer information. Microsoft Access, FileMaker Pro, and OpenOffice Base are examples of database programs for personal computers.

FIGURE C-27: Creating a table in Microsoft Access

Used with permission from Microsoft

Each row is a record   Enter data in each field   Enter field names   Specify the type of data the field will hold

● **What is presentation software?** **Presentation software** provides the tools you need for combining text, graphics, graphs, animations, video, and sound into a series of electronic slides. See Figure C-28. You can display the electronic slides on a monitor for a one-on-one presentation, or you can use a computer projection device for group presentations. On-screen tools such as the highlighter or pen make it possible for you to annotate the slide during the presentation. How the slides advance is up to you. You can have the slides display automatically at set intervals, or you can advance the slides manually. Transitions between slides, such as checkerboard or wipes, create dramatic effect. You can also output the presentation as overhead transparencies, paper copies of the slides with or without notes, or 35-mm slides. Microsoft PowerPoint, iWork Keynote, and OpenOffice Impress are examples of presentation software programs.

FIGURE C-28: A slide in a Microsoft PowerPoint presentation

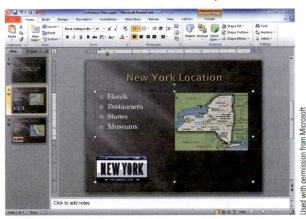

Used with permission from Microsoft

Other productivity software

Word processing, spreadsheet, database, presentation, and scheduling software are the five main types of office productivity software. Scheduling software such as Microsoft Outlook includes an email program. Two other office productivity software include Web authoring and desktop publishing software.

Web authoring software helps you design and develop Web pages that can be published on the Web. Web authoring software provides tools for generating HTML tags, which is the code used to display a document on the Web.

Desktop publishing (DTP) software provides both word processing and graphic design tools. Many of today's word processing programs offer page layout and design features. However, desktop publishing programs, such as Microsoft Publisher (Figure C-29), provide more sophisticated features to help you produce professional-quality publications. Most word processing software is page-oriented, meaning that it treats each page as a rectangle that can be filled with text and graphics. Text automatically flows from one page to the next. In contrast, most DTP software is frame-oriented, allowing you to divide each

page into several rectangular-shaped frames that you can fill with text or graphics. Text flows from one frame to the next. You will want to use DTP to create complex documents, such as marketing brochures or magazines.

FIGURE C-29: A page created using Microsoft Publisher

Used with permission from Microsoft

Graphics Software

You may want to include images, such as digital photos or pictures you draw using the computer, in your work. These images are called graphics. The term **graphics** refers to any picture, drawing, sketch, photograph, image, or icon that appears on your computer screen or on your printed output. **Graphics software** is designed to help you create, display, modify, manipulate, and print graphics. Many kinds of graphics software are available, and each one is typically used with a particular type of graphic. Individuals who work with graphics will undoubtedly use more than one graphics program.

Learning Objective 8:
Define graphics software, and name examples in each major category

● **Can I use my computer to draw or create graphic images?** Yes. You can use **paint software** (sometimes called **image editing software**) to create more sophisticated images. Paint software provides a set of electronic pens, brushes, and paints for painting images on the screen. You can create these images from scratch, or you can use an existing image or photograph and add your own touches. See Figure C-30. A simple program called Microsoft Paint is included with Windows. More sophisticated paint programs include Corel Paint Shop Pro and Adobe Photoshop.

FIGURE C-30: Paint software

Used with permission from Microsoft

Tools on the Ribbon   Different brushes   Drawing canvas

You can also use **drawing software**, which provides tools, such as a set of lines, shapes, and colors. You can use these tools to create simple images, such as diagrams and corporate logos. The drawings created with drawing software, such as Adobe Illustrator and CorelDraw, tend

to have a flat cartoonlike quality, but they are very easy to modify and look good at just about any size.

● **Can I use my computer to edit my digital photographs?** Yes. You can use **photo editing software**, such as Adobe Photoshop and Corel PaintShop Pro. These programs include features that help you improve the quality of your photos. For example, using photo editing software, you can modify an image's contrast and brightness, crop unwanted objects, and remove "red eye." These programs often include photo organizers to help you locate and categorize your photos. See Figure C-31. Although photos can be edited using paint software, photo editing software typically provides tools that simplify common photo editing tasks.

FIGURE C-31: Photo editing software

Screenshot is © Copyright 2011 Corel Corporation and Corel Corporation Limited, reprinted by permission. Image courtesy of Rachel B. Bunin

● **Is there a quick way to include art in my document?** You have several options. First, you can use clip art in your document, presentation, spreadsheet, or even database table. **Clip art** is a collection of graphic images. These images might be drawn images or they might be photographs. These images are readily available. They are often included with some office productivity software. See Figure C-32. When using one of the Microsoft Office productivity programs, open the Clip Art task pane, and then search on a keyword to find an image that meets your needs.

FIGURE C-32: Inserting clip art in a presentation

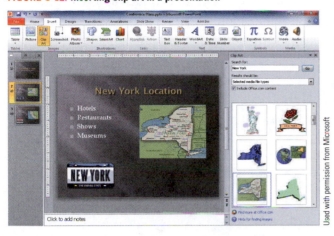

Collections of clip art focused on a particular theme can be purchased at a store or downloaded from a Web site. You can use your favorite search engine to find a wide variety of clip art that is ready to be inserted into your document. Before using any clip art, be sure to review its acceptable use statement to ensure you do not violate its copyright laws.

In addition to clip art, you can scan images, such as photographs, using a scanner. Once the image is scanned and saved, you have an electronic file of that image. You can insert that image and manipulate it in your document in the same way you would insert any picture in a document.

● **What software can I use to create three-dimensional graphics?** You can use 3D graphics software to create 3D graphics. **3D graphics software** provides a set of tools for creating wire-frame models that represent three-dimensional objects. A wire-frame model is similar to the frame for a pop-up tent. In much the same way that you would construct the frame for the tent and then cover it with nylon fabric, you can use a 3D graphics program to cover a wire-frame model with surface texture and color to create a graphic of a 3D object. See Figure C-33.

FIGURE C-33: 3D graphics created using software programs

● **What software is used to create technical drawings or blueprints? CAD (computer-aided design)** software is a special type of 3D graphics software. It is used by architects, engineers, and others who use computers to create blueprints and product specifications. You can purchase scaled-down versions of professional CAD programs. These programs provide simplified tools you can use for tasks such as redesigning your kitchen or drawing up new landscaping options. You may have used a CAD program at a home improvement store, where CAD is used to help customers visualize home improvement designs.

● **Do movie studios use computers to create graphics in films?** Computers and 3D graphics software are used extensively in the movie industry. Feature-length 3D animated films are responsible for stunning technology breakthroughs, such as the ability to realistically depict the movement of clothing on a moving animated character and animate individual strands of hair or fur. Graphics design companies such as Pixar Animation Studios and DreamWorks use 3D animation techniques to produce animated feature films as well as special effects.

Using data responsibly

Data can be numbers, text, or images. Whether you print, import, copy, save, or transmit the data in databases, worksheets, or documents, it is your responsibility to use the data appropriately. Here are some simple guidelines you can follow at work, home, or school to help you toward this effort. You should never introduce inaccurate information into a database, worksheet, or document. You should never alter the data in any way, such as to digitally change a photograph or substitute words in a quotation. You should always respect copyrights and always be sure to give credit to the person or organization that compiled the data. You should always respect the privacy of the people who are the subject of the data. Unless you have permission to do so, do not divulge names, Social Security numbers, or other identifying information that might compromise someone's privacy.

Other Application Software

In addition to office productivity and graphics software, there are many other categories of application software. Some of the major categories are entertainment, gaming, music and video, education, business, and science. Application software in these categories can help you use your computer for entertainment, such as listening to music, playing games, and watching videos. They can help you use your computer for number-crunching tasks such as money management, mathematical modeling, or statistical analysis. This lesson looks at just a few of the many other types of application software.

Learning Objective 9:
Name other categories of application software, and give examples in each major category

● **Can I use my computer to play games?** Yes. Computer games are the most popular type of entertainment software. Computer games are generally classified into subcategories, such as simulations, multiplayer, role-playing, action, adventure, puzzles, and strategy/war games. Some games use game controllers that simulate musical intruments to interact with a computer. See Figure C-34. For example, you can use a guitar game controller to play lead guitar, bass guitar, and rhythm guitar across numerous rock music songs. Multiplayer games provide an environment in which two or more players can participate in the same game. Players can use Internet technology to band together in sophisticated virtual environments. Large-scale multiplayer games operate on multiple Internet servers, each one with the capacity to handle thousands of players at peak times.

FIGURE C-34: Playing a computer game

© Dooley Productions/Shutterstock.com

● **Can I use my computer to create music and sound?** You can use **audio editing software** to make digital voice and music recordings. You can store these files on your computer. Audio editing software typically includes playback as well as recording capabilities so you can preview your work and make changes as needed. Your operating system might supply audio editing software, such as Sound Recorder, or you can download open source software, such as Audacity. See Figure C-35.

Ear training software targets musicians and music students who want to learn to play by ear, develop tuning skills,

FIGURE C-35: Audio editing software

"Audacity" is a trademark of Dominic Mazzoni

Rewind to beginning   Play   Record   Stop   Fast forward to end

recognize notes and keys, and develop other musical skills. Notation software is the musician's equivalent of a word processor. It helps musicians compose, edit, and print the notes for their compositions. For non-musicians, **computer-aided music software** is designed to generate unique musical compositions simply by selecting the musical style, instruments, key, and tempo. MIDI sequencing software and software synthesizers are great for sound effects and for controlling keyboards and other digital instruments.

● **Can I use my computer to edit and create videos?** Yes. You can use **video editing software** and **DVD authoring software**. These programs provide tools for transferring video footage from a camcorder to a computer, deleting unwanted footage, assembling video segments in any sequence, adding special visual effects, and adding a sound track. See Figure C-36. Video editing software allows desktop video authors to transfer their productions to DVDs and watch them on standard DVD players connected to television sets or projectors. Just like commercial movies, desktop videos can now include menu selections, such as Play Movie, Scene Selection, and Special Features.

FIGURE C-36: Video editing software

Used with permission from Microsoft; Courtesy of MediaTechnics Corporation

Preview your video to see how the clips, transitions, and soundtrack all work together

Add titles and transitions

Arrange the audio tracks to synchronize with each video clip

Import video clips, crop the footage, and arrange it in any order

● **How can I use my computer to learn new skills?**
You can use **educational software** to learn and practice new skills. For the youngest students, this software can be used to reinforce basic skills. Instruction is presented in game format, and the level of play is adapted to the player's age and ability. When educational software is also entertaining, it is called **edutainment software.** For older students and adults, software is available to teach new skills, such as a foreign language, or to improve existing skills, such as keyboarding skills. **Reference software** spans a wide range of applications from encyclopedias and medical references to map software, trip planners, cookbooks, and telephone books. To find information in a reference program, you can search using keywords or you can click hyperlinks to access related articles.

● **What software is used to track business projects?**
Project management software, such as Microsoft Project, is an important tool for planning and managing large or small projects. The software helps you with scheduling the project, assigning project tasks, tracking and allocating resources, and keeping an eye on project costs. See Figure C-37. Project management software is used to report progress and an overview of the project at any point to the main stakeholders and managers of a project.

FIGURE C-37: Project management software

Used with permission from Microsoft

● **What software is used to manage business finances?** **Accounting software** and **finance software** is used to keep a record of monetary transactions and investments. See Figure C-38. These easy-to-use programs do not require more than a basic understanding of accounting and finance principles. This type of software helps you invoice customers and keep track of what they owe. It stores additional customer data, such as contact information and purchasing history. Inventory functions keep track of the products that you carry. Payroll capabilities automatically calculate wages and deduct federal, state, and local taxes. **Tax preparation software** is a specialized type of **personal finance software** designed to help organize your annual income and expense data, identify deductions, and calculate your tax payment.

FIGURE C-38: An example of finance software

Courtesy of Intuit Inc.

● **Is there software specifically designed to analyze data?** Yes. **Mathematical modeling software**, such as MathCAD and Mathematica, provides tools for solving a wide range of math, science, and engineering problems. Students, teachers, mathematicians, and engineers like how this software helps them see patterns that can be difficult to identify in columns of numbers.

You can use **statistical software** to analyze large sets of data in order to discover relationships and patterns. Statistical software is a helpful tool for summarizing survey results, test scores, experiment results, or population data. Most statistical software includes graphing capability so that data can be displayed and explored visually.

Talking Points: What Is The Downside To Software Piracy?

Software is easy to steal. For example, a customer does not have to walk out of a Staples or Best Buy store with a Quicken Deluxe box under his or her shirt to steal the program. Instead, the individual can simply borrow a friend's distribution discs and install a copy of the program on his or her computer's hard drive. Software piracy seems so simple that it could not be illegal; but it is! Software piracy takes many forms. Examples of end-user piracy include friends loaning distribution discs to each other and installing software on more computers than the license allows.

> **"Counterfeit software is sold in retail stores and online auctions—often the packaging looks so authentic that buyers have no idea they have purchased illegal goods."**

Counterfeiting is the large-scale illegal duplication of software distribution media and sometimes even its packaging. According to Microsoft, many software counterfeiting groups are linked to organized crime and money-laundering schemes that fund a diverse collection of illegal activities. Counterfeit software is sold in retail stores and online auctions—often the packaging looks so authentic that buyers have no idea they have purchased illegal goods.

Internet piracy uses the Web as a way to distribute unauthorized software illegally. Some pirated software has even been modified to eliminate serial numbers, registration requirements, expiration dates, or other forms of copy protection. Web sites, peer-to-peer file sharing networks, and auction sites sell or distribute hundreds of thousands of pirated software products. In many countries, including the United States, software pirates are subject to civil lawsuits for monetary damages and criminal prosecution, which can result in jail time and stiff fines. Nonetheless, software piracy continues to have enormous impact.

According to a Business Software Alliance (BSA) and IDC Piracy Study, $130 billion dollars of software was legitimately purchased worldwide, but software worth a whopping $53 billion dollars was pirated. Figure C-39 shows piracy rates by region.

There is good news in this study, however. Progress was seen in a number of emerging markets, most notably in China, In China the piracy rate is 79%, down from 92% in 2003. In the

FIGURE C-39: Results of BSA/IDC Global Software Piracy study

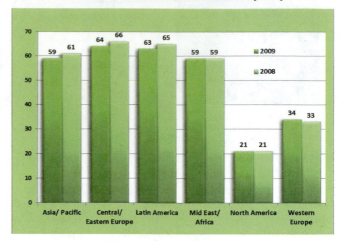

Source: Seventh Annual BSA/IDC Global Software Piracy Study

United States, an estimated 20% of software is pirated. In Japan, the rate is 21%.

As justification for high piracy rates, some observers point out that people in many countries simply cannot afford software priced for the U.S. market. This argument could apply to China, where the average annual income is equivalent to about US $5,420, and to North Korea, where the average income is only US $2,820. A Korean who legitimately purchases Microsoft Office for US $250 would be spending about one-tenth of his or her annual income. Annual income rates do not necessarily correlate with piracy, however. Most countries with a high incidence of software piracy have strong economies and respectable per capita incomes. To further discredit the theory that piracy stems from poverty, India—which has a fairly large computer-user community, but a per capita income of only US $2,740—is not among the top 20 countries with high rates of software piracy.

Analysts believe that the Internet is a major factor in piracy growth. In fact, access to high-speed Internet connections makes it much easier to download large software files quickly.

Why should you care if someone uses Microsoft Office without paying for it? Is software piracy really damaging? Yes, without a doubt, it is damaging. Software piracy is damaging because it has a negative effect on the economy. Software production makes a major contribution to the United States economy, employing more than two million people and accounting for billions of dollars in corporate revenue. Software piracy in the

United States is responsible for tens of thousands of lost jobs, millions in lost wages, and lost tax revenues. A BSA economic impact study concluded that lowering global piracy from an average of 35% to only 25% would add more than 600,000 jobs and $141 billion in worldwide economic growth.

Decreases in software revenues can have a direct effect on consumers, too. When software publishers must cut corners, they tend to reduce customer service and technical support. As a result, you, the consumer, get put on hold when you call for technical support, find fewer free technical support sites, and encounter customer support personnel who are only moderately knowledgeable about their products. The bottom line—software piracy negatively affects customer service.

As an alternative to cutting support costs, some software publishers might build the cost of software piracy into the price of the software. The unfortunate result is that those who legitimately license and purchase software pay an inflated price.

The Software & Information Industry Association (SIIA) is an association for software companies whose mission is to protect, promote, and inform the industry. Part of its mission is to fight software piracy. See Figure C-40. To help with that effort, the SIIA provides an online form, as well as a toll-free number, for reporting piracy. SIIA also works hard to educate the consumer about piracy and its effects.

FIGURE C-40: SIIA Logos

Courtesy of the Software & Information Industry Association

Some analysts suggest that people need more education about software copyrights and the economic implications of piracy. Other analysts believe that copyright enforcement must be increased by implementing more vigorous efforts to identify and prosecute pirates.

> **As an alternative to cutting support costs, some software publishers might build the cost of software piracy into the price of the software. The unfortunate result is that those who legitimately license and purchase software pay an inflated price.**

Expand the Ideas

1. Do you believe that software piracy is a serious issue? Write a two-page paper supporting your position. Include the opposing side's arguments in your report. Be sure to include your resources.

2. Do you think there are ways that software publishers can control piracy in the United States? In other countries? Do you know of any recent attempts at doing so? Work in a small group to brainstorm ideas and research recent trends or events. Compile your ideas and findings into a short presentation to give to the class. Include handouts for the audience and cite any sources you used.

3. Do you think that most software pirates understand that what they are doing is illegal? Design a marketing campaign that could be used to educate the public about the issue. Create a poster that could be used in the campaign.

4. Should software publishers try to adjust software pricing for local markets? How would you propose such a pricing structure? How would these policies be enforced? Can you think of any other industry that adjusts prices for local markets? Write a two-page paper discussing your proposals and explaining your findings. Be sure to cite your sources.

Software marketing and reviews

New software comes on the market frequently. At times, it can seem impossible to keep up with the flow of new software. However, publications and Web sites can help you keep up to date regarding software developments that might improve your computing experience.

Computer and technology magazines, such as *Wired*, *Macworld*, and *PC Magazine*, usually include software reviews in every issue. Most computer magazines have companion Web sites and some of those significantly extend the material offered in the magazine's printed pages. ZDNet and CNET (reviews.cnet.com),

for example, offer in-depth comparison reviews written by experts and tested under laboratory conditions.

Consumer-oriented Web sites also offer reviews. For example, the site toptenreviews.com contains easy-to-understand, in-depth checklists that make it easy to compare the features of popular software packages. User reviews and ratings can be found at download sites, such as download.com, cnet.com, as well as at comparison shopping sites, including bizrate.com, Amazon.com, and newegg.com. You might also find a blog or news feed that focuses on the type of software you typically use.

Key Terms & Unit Review

Key Terms

3D graphics software
Accounting software
App
Application software
Audo editing software
Boot process
Buffer
CAD (computer-aided design) software
Clip art
Cloudware
Commercial software
Compression utility
Computer-aided music software
Computer program
Concurrent-use license
Copyright
Copyright notice
Digital content
Database
Database software
Demoware
Desktop gadget
Desktop publishing software

Device driver
Drawing software
DVD authoring software
Educational software
Edutainment software
EULA (end-user license agreement)
Finance software
Freeware
Gadget
General Public License (GPL)
Graphical user interface (GUI)
Graphics
Graphics software
Image editing software
Installation agreement
Intellectual property
License agreement
Linux
Local application
Mac OS
Mathematical modeling software
Mobile application
Multiple-user license

Multitasking
Office productivity software
Open source software
Operating system (OS)
Paint software
Patch
Personal finance software
Photo editing software
Pirated software
Portable application
Presentation software
Productivity software
Project management software
Proprietary software
Public domain software
Reference software
Resource
Restore point
Security utility
Service pack
Setup program
Shareware
Shrink-wrap license
Single-user license

Site license
Software
Software license
Software pirate
Software suite
Software upgrade
Spreadsheet software
Statistical software
System requirements
System software
Tax preparation software
User interface
Utility software (utilities)
Validation code
Video editing software
Web app
Web application
Web authoring software
Widget
Windows
Word processing software
Worksheet

Unit Review

1. Use your own words to define each of the bold terms that appear throughout the unit. List ten of the terms that are the least familiar to you and write a sentence for each of them.

2. List at least five categories of application software and give an example of how you might use each type.

3. Explain the single-user, site license, multiple-user, and concurrent-user software licenses described in this unit.

4. In your own words, explain shareware, freeware, demoware, and open source software.

5. Describe the main activities you must perform when you install software on your computer. Explain the differences between downloaded software and software you buy in a store.

6. List three features of the Windows operating system discussed in this unit. Write a brief summary of each feature.

7. Name three resources managed by an operating system.

8. List three types of office productivity software that you might use, and describe how you might use each one.

9. List three types of software that you might use for creating and editing graphics, and describe how you might use each one.

10. Create a list of three utilities described in this unit and give an example of why you would use each one on the list.

Concepts Review

Select the best answer.

1. Software can be divided into two major categories: system software and _____ software.
   - a. Web app
   - b. application
   - c. utility
   - d. security

2. You should use _____ software for numerical calculations, such as tracking income and expenses.
   - a. spreadsheet
   - b. database
   - c. document production
   - d. utility

3. A software _____ is a collection of application software sold as a single package.
   - a. operating system
   - b. DVD
   - c. suite
   - d. productivity program

4. A(n) _____ is utility software that helps a peripheral device communicate with a computer.
   - a. operating system
   - b. desktop gadget
   - c. connector
   - d. device driver

5. To run more than one program at a time, the _____ must allocate specific areas of memory for each program.
   - a. RAM
   - b. operating system
   - c. device driver
   - d. ROM

6. When _____ software is used, program files do not exist on the hard drive and no configuration data is stored on the hard drive.
   - a. demoware
   - b. database
   - c. portable
   - d. freeware

7. _____ is distributed under the terms of a General Public License (GPL), which allows everyone to make copies for his or her own use, to give it to others, or to sell it.
   - a. Linux
   - b. Windows
   - c. Mac OS
   - d. Office

8. When using Windows, you can open the _____ Manager to see a list of processes that are being executed by the processor.
   - a. Windows
   - b. Program
   - c. Explorer
   - d. Task

9. The three main operating systems running most personal computers today are _____, Mac OS, and Linux.
   - a. FileZilla
   - b. Windows
   - c. Office
   - d. Internet Explorer

10. You can use _____ software to help organize information, such as library books and contacts.
    - a. database
    - b. spreadsheet
    - c. document production
    - d. finance and accounting

11. A desktop _____ is a utility program that may provide information, such as the weather or a calendar.
    - a. icon
    - b. gadget
    - c. task
    - d. menu

12. _____ software is a special type of 3D graphics software designed for architects and engineers who use computers to create blueprints and product specifications.
    - a. DTP
    - b. Statistical
    - c. CAD
    - d. Product Management

13. As part of the _____ program, you might be asked what type of installation you want: full or custom.
    - a. Web app
    - b. license
    - c. setup
    - d. demoware

14. To read a Portable Document File (PDF), you need to use _____ software.
    - a. Microsoft Excel
    - b. Microsoft Word
    - c. OpenOffice Document
    - d. Adobe Reader

15. To combat piracy, many software publishers require users to type in a(n) _____ code, a sequence of numbers and letters in order to complete an installation.
    - a. EULA
    - b. validation
    - c. private
    - d. pass

16. Snow Leopard, Cheetah, Puma, Jaguar, Panther, Tiger, and Leopard are all examples of _____.
    - a. Windows programs
    - b. Apple OSs
    - c. license agreements
    - d. Smartphone OSs

17. _____ laws provide software authors with the exclusive right to copy, distribute, sell, and modify their work, except under special circumstances.
    - a. Copyright
    - b. Software
    - c. Shareware
    - d. Piracy

18. _____ is copyrighted software that is marketed with a try-before-you-buy policy.
    - a. Demoware
    - b. Freeware
    - c. Utility software
    - d. Shareware

19. A(n) _____ license is priced at a flat rate so software can be used on all computers at a specific location.
    - a. Single-user
    - b. Shareware
    - c. Multi-user
    - d. Demoware

20. _____ software is not copyrighted, making it available for use without restriction, except that you cannot apply for a copyright on it.
    - a. Demoware
    - b. Productivity
    - c. Public Domain
    - d. Commercial

Independent Challenges

Independent Challenge 1

There are many software packages on the market today. Software is often dictated by the computer you are using and the installed operating system. Operating systems are updated every few years, giving you more options for newer features and new software.

Application software is also updated regularly. In addition, new programs come on the market frequently. In fact, the amount of software available in each category can be overwhelming, and no two packages offer all the same features. How can you make a decision about which software you need? How do you know which software to buy? Do you follow recommendations received by word of mouth? Do you read reviewer comments in professional magazines? Do you simply try it out? Do you go to the Web and find a software superstore and read all the reviews and descriptions? See Figure C-41.

FIGURE C-41: Software superstore

© Jorg Hackemann/Shutterstock.com

For this Independent Challenge:

Write a short summary answering each of the questions that follow.

1. Which operating system do you use?

2. What software is installed on your computer? How did you acquire the software? How would you categorize each program?

3. Identify one software program you want to download to your computer, such as an office productivity, a graphics, a Web development, an email, or a utility program. Locate vendor ads either on the Internet or in local papers or trade magazines that sell or discuss that program. Find two competitive products for the program you want to buy. Read comparison reviews of the products. Create a chart detailing the features and prepare a competitive analysis of the two products.

4. What are the system requirements for each program? Does your computer meet those requirements?

5. What kind of software license is required by each program? Do you have to pay for using it? Can you try it first, then pay after a trial period? Do you understand the licensing agreement? Write a short summary of your findings, indicating which program you would buy and why.

Independent Challenge 2

Copyrights and software piracy are relevant issues for software users, developers, businesspeople, and educators. There is constant debate among all stakeholders as to the best models for software distribution, as well as how developers, publishers, or programmers should be compensated.

For this Independent Challenge:

1. Log onto the Internet and use your favorite search engine to search for Web sites that discuss software piracy. Using information you have gathered through your research, select one of the following viewpoints and argue for or against it.

Discuss the topic of software piracy from the perspective of one of the following: a.) an advocate who believes in free software for all, b.) a librarian who believes that copyright laws, especially the Digital Millennium Copyright Act, minimize the needs of the public and go too far in their efforts to protect the rights of software authors, c.) a member of the Software Publishers Association who believes all software is protected by copyright law and the consumer should purchase all software and abide by the EULA.

2. Select one of the perspectives listed above or state your own perspective, then write a two- to five-page paper about this issue, based on information you gather from the Internet.

3. Be sure to cite your sources and list them as part of the paper.

4. Follow your instructor's directions for formatting and submitting your paper.

Independent Challenge 3

Smartphones and tablet computers are becoming the digital device of choice. Most people are turning in their cell phones to upgrade to smartphones with a data plan. As a result, more and more mobile apps are being developed to meet the growing consumer demand. Currently, there are apps that exist for fun and games. There are apps to help people navigate through their day. And, there are apps that are just silly. Whether or not you own a smartphone or a tablet computer now, you probably know at least one person who does. Learning about smartphones and tablets, as well as the mobile apps becoming so popular today, provides insight into the world of mobile computing.

For this Independent Challenge:

1. Log onto the Internet and search for information on the following mobile operating systems: Windows Phone, Android, iOS.

   Complete the chart shown in Table C-3 to learn more about each of the operating systems.

2. Go to a Web site that features Android apps, such as the Android market shown in Figure C-42. Explore the offerings and the different categories then answer the following questions:
   a. What is the most interesting free app that you can find to download? Why would you want this app? What made you select this app?

FIGURE C-42: Android market

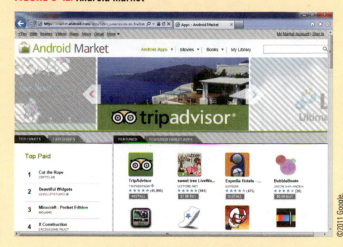

©2011 Google.

   b. What is the most interesting app that you have to pay for? Why would you want this app? Why do you think it is worth paying for this app rather than getting a different free app?

3. Go to a Web site that features apps for Apple tablets or smartphones. Explore the offerings then answer the following questions:
   a. What is the most interesting free app that you can find to download? Why would you want this app?
   b. What is the most interesting app that you have to pay for? Why would you want this app? Why do you think it is worth paying for this app rather than getting a different free app?

TABLE C-3: Comparison chart

	Windows Phone	Android	iOS
Current version			
Latest features mentioned most in the marketing			
Three digital devices that can be purchased with this OS preinstalled			
Two game apps			
Two productivity apps			
One surprising fact			

© Cengage Learning

Guide to Buying a Computer

As you prepare to buy a computer, there are many decisions you have to make. This book is designed to help you build the knowledge base you need to purchase a computer, and then buy and install software on that computer. In this unit, you were introduced to the basics of the operating system and the different types of application software and utilities you might need to buy for your computer. Some software is provided with the operating system. Office productivity software can be expensive. However, you can take advantage of student discounts, competitive pricing, and various licensing options.

To be able to make decisions regarding buying a computer and the software you need, you have to do your homework. As an informed consumer, you should be aware of your options, research different software publishers, and compare features of each package. Computer and technology magazines, such as *Wired*, *Macworld*, and *PC Magazine*, usually include software reviews in every issue. Most computer magazines have companion Web sites and some of those significantly extend the material offered in the magazine's printed pages.

To help you organize the information you will need when you are ready to buy a computer, you should complete the following activities.

1. Research three productivity programs and three utility programs you might need. List the programs you selected, the cost, and a site where you read a review of each program. State whether you will buy the program or not.

   _____

   _____

   _____

   _____

   _____

   _____

2. Explore the idea of purchasing a software suite instead of individual software programs. Compare two productivity software suites, such as OpenOffice with Microsoft Office. What were the differences in features between the two software suites? What are the costs for each? Do you think the values are comparable?

   _____

   _____

   _____

   _____

3. Computers can help you perform such a wide variety of tasks that it can be impossible to predict all the ways you might use your new machine in the future. You can, however, make a list of the ways you plan to immediately use your computer and that list can help you think about the software you'll need. List some of the ways below.

   _____

   _____

Deciding whether to buy boxed software or download software

Boxed software can be purchased in a store or shipped to you by mail. The box usually includes distribution CDs and an installation manual. It might also include a user manual, but many software publishers supply user manuals online. The advantage of distribution CDs is their availability in case your hard drive fails and you have to reinstall your software. Boxed software can give you a physical record of your registration code, serial number, and certificate of authenticity, which might be necessary for reinstallation.

You can download software from a Web site instead of buying it in a box. Downloading can be convenient. It saves you a trip to the store and you don't have to wait for a mail order package to arrive. Depending on the speed of your Internet connection, however, downloads can tie up your computer for a few hours. Even with a fast connection a download can be interrupted and you might have to call customer service to restart it without paying for the product again. Downloading can be risky. Some download sites display an irritating number of ads and are sometimes exploited by hackers. Software downloaded from less reputable sites might contain viruses. When possible you should download directly from the software publisher's Web site or from a download site operated by a reputable business, such as a computer magazine or retailer. In any case, it is good practice to scan downloaded files for viruses before installing them.

Prices for boxed software and Web downloads can vary, so if you have the time to shop around, you are likely to save some money.

4. As you continue to work through this book, you will learn more about personal computer systems. You will have the opportunity to answer more questions and complete other worksheets with information that will help you when it is time to buy a computer. To help you think about the software you need, fill in this portion of the Guide to Buying a Computer worksheet. Try to list the name of specific software programs you might buy or you would like to review further for each answer in the Notes column.

Guide to Buying a Computer: Getting started

Questions to consider	Pages where the topic is covered in this book (refer back to these pages to read more about the topic)	Notes (add additional comments, clarifications, or ideas about each topic)
Which operating system do you want?		
If you are considering Windows, which edition should you get?		
What browser are you considering?		
Do you plan to create documents? If so, what word processing program do you plan to use?		
Will you need to work with numbers? If so, what spreadsheet program or other numeric software do you plan to use?		
Will you need to create computer slide shows or presentations? If so, what presentation program do you plan to use?		
Will you need to work with graphics, such as original computer art? If so, what graphics program do you plan to use?		
Will you want to edit or organize photographs? If so, what image editing program do you plan to use?		
Are you going to use your computer to listen to music? To transfer music to your MP3 player? If so, what programs will you need? Do you need to consider any special hardware as well?		
What utility software will you need? Will you want to send compressed files? Customize your desktop? Maintain your disk's health?		
Rather than buying all individual programs, are there any software suites you might consider?		
What type of licensing works best for you for the software that you plan to buy?		
Do you have a tablet or smartphone? If yes, what do you use these devices for on a daily basis?		
What apps do you have on the mobile digital device? Do you plan to purchase any apps for your digital device? If so, which type? Any specific apps?		

Visual Workshop

Mobile devices, such as tablet computers and smartphones now have the ability, through software and the different networks, to allow you to video chat or conference with other people directly from your device. Popular video chatting services include Tango, Fring, FaceTime, GoogleChat, and Skype. Figure C-43 shows the Tango home page. You will compare and contrast each option on its basic features.

FIGURE C-43: Mobile video chatting

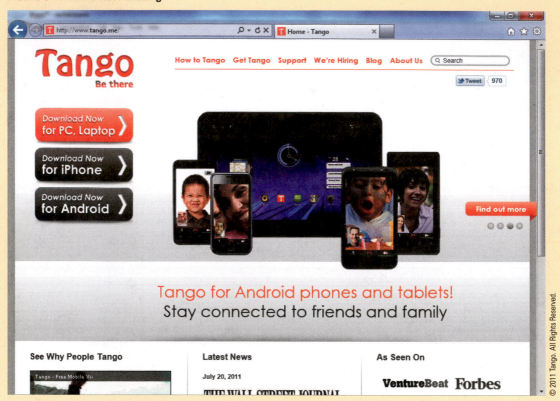

Log onto the Internet. Find Web sites that discuss each of these video chatting services listed above.

1. In your research, find three facts about each of the competing services.

2. What are the purchasing options, fees, and licensing options for each?

3. What operating systems are required for each? Are there limitations?

4. Which devices are supported by each of these video chatting services?

5. Are any interesting features built into these video chatting services?

File Management and Digital Electronics

Learning Objectives

1. Explain how file management programs help you manage your computer files
2. Explain how to create and use folders to store files
3. Identify the key elements of a computer file
4. Describe the file management steps for working with files
5. Describe how digital data representation produces numbers, text, images, video, and sound
6. Define integrated circuits and explain the role they play inside a computer
7. Explain how CPU factors affect computer performance
8. Define RAM and explain its importance to computers
9. Explain how a computer uses virtual memory, ROM, and EEPROM

LESSON TOPICS

- File Management Tools
- Computer Folder Basics
- Computer File Basics
- How to Manage Computer Files
- How Computers Represent Data
- Integrated Circuits—An Overview
- Processors—An Overview
- Computer Memory: RAM
- Other Types of Computer Memory

Talking Points: Is Your Computer Making You Sick?

Courtesy of Emily Bunin

File Management Tools

A typical personal computer stores thousands of computer files, usually in folders. You use file management tools to manage your files and folders. To organize your computer files and folders, you need to practice good **file management**. Good file management practices include how you create, open, save, delete, and rename files.

Learning Objective 1:
Explain how file management programs help you manage your computer files

- **What is a computer file?** A computer file, or simply file, is defined as a named collection of data that exists on a storage medium. The storage medium can be a hard drive, solid-state storage device, CD, DVD, BD, or tape. The content of the file is determined by the software program used to create the file and the data you enter. For example, you can use a word processing program to create a document file for your résumé.

- **What is a folder?** A **folder** is a logical representation of where you store your files on a computer. Folders help you organize your computer files.

- **How do folders help me organize my files?** By storing files in folders, you assign each file a place in a hierarchy of folders. Think of a data storage system as a filing cabinet. See Figure D-1. Each storage device is a drawer in a filing cabinet. Just like the drawers in a filing cabinet, a storage device is made up of folders and the folders hold files.

FIGURE D-1: Files are stored in folders

File cabinet storage   Computer file storage

© Cengage Learning; Used with permission from Microsoft

The file cabinet is a useful way to visualize how files and folders are organized on a storage device. The drive, folder names, and filename all work together to identify the file path.

- **What is a file path?** The location of a file on a storage device is defined by its **file path** (also called **file specification**). The file path begins with the drive letter and is followed by the folder(s), filename, and file extension. A folder name is separated from a drive letter and other folder names by a special

symbol. In Windows, this symbol is often represented on screen as an arrow head and written as the backslash (\ ). For example, the path to the folder Sarah uses to store Elvis music would be C:\Users\Sarah\My Music\Elvis\Hound Dog.mp3. This path tells you that Sarah stored an MP3 file called Hound Dog in the Elvis folder in the My Music folder on her hard drive. Its file path is shown in Figure D-2.

FIGURE D-2: A file path

C:\Users\Sarah\My Music\Elvis\Hound Dog.mp3

| Primary folder | Subfolder | Subfolder | Subfolder | Filename | File extension |

© Cengage Learning

- **Who decides where my files are stored?** You decide where your files are stored. But to help you, Windows supplies a series of default locations. These locations include the four Libraries as well as default folders. See Figure D-3.

FIGURE D-3: Windows default folders

Used with permission from Microsoft

- **What is a library?** A **library** contains a set of links to similar files that are stored on various devices and in various folders. A library is similar to a folder. When you open a library in **Windows Explorer**, you'll see one or more folders and files. A library does not actually store files, but rather provides a view of the files. A library can display folders that are found in several locations. A library can give you access to files and folders on your hard drive, an external drive, and also folders that have been shared over a network. You cannot use a library for removable storage such as a flash drive. In Windows 7, there are four default libraries: Documents, Music, Pictures, and Videos.

- **Where are my files stored if they are not stored in the libraries?** Your files are stored at the location you specify. For example, when you save a data file, you specify the location where you want to save the file. The default location for a file such as a letter or spreadsheet is the My Documents folder. The Document library tracks the saved file and you can access it through the library as needed. You can save your file to a default folder, or you can create a new folder and save your file to the new folder. However, avoid storing files in the root directory of your hard drive. Files should be stored in subfolders in the root directory.

  When you install a program, the installation process usually creates a new folder within the default Programs folder. This folder is not tracked by any of the libraries. Although you can change the suggested location when you install a software program, it is recommended that you don't.

- **What is the root directory?** The **root directory** is the main directory of the hard drive or other storage medium. So for a hard drive named C:, the root directory is also C:.

- **Do I name the root directory?** No, the root directory is the name of your storage device and it is assigned by your operating system. For example, the Windows operating system labels storage devices with letters, such as A: and C:. See Figure D-4.

A device letter is usually followed by a colon. The main hard drive is usually referred to as drive C or as Local Disk (C:). Additional storage devices can be assigned letters from D through Z.

The device letters for additional storage devices are not standardized. As a result, the file path for a file can change. For example, if you store a data file on a flash drive, the file path for the file will include the drive letter for the flash drive. The drive letter is based on which computer the flash drive is connected to. If you remove the flash drive and insert it in a new computer, the flash drive is assigned a new drive letter based on that computer. So, the file specification for a file might be F:\Cards\Birthday1.docx on a flash drive connected to one computer, but the file path for that same file might be H:\Cards\Birthday1.docx on the same flash drive connected to a different computer.

- **What should I use to manage the files on my computer?** Most operating systems provide a **file management program**. These programs contain the tools you need to organize your files. For computers running Windows, the file management program is called Windows Explorer. Using Windows Explorer, you can see the storage devices and a list of files and folders on those storage devices or on your network. You can find files, move files, make copies of files, delete files, view file properties, and rename files. Figure D-5 shows the Windows Explorer window.

  In addition, a file management program makes it easy to find the file or folder you are looking for by using the program's search capabilities. *TIP:* Do not confuse Windows Explorer (file management program) with Internet Explorer (a browser program you use to view Web sites on the Internet).

FIGURE D-4: Storage devices labeled with letters

Used with permission from Microsoft

FIGURE D-5: Windows Explorer showing contents of Sample Music folder

Used with permission from Microsoft

Hierarchy of devices and folders

Details pane for selected file

Selected folder

Contents of selected folder

Computer and Internet Basics

Computer Folder Basics

A folder is a logical representation of where you store your files on a computer. For example, you can use a folder called My Documents to hold reports, budgets, letters, and so on. If you understand how to use and manage folders, you will be able to organize the files on your computer successfully.

> ## Learning Objective 2:
> Explain how to create and use folders to store files

- **Why should I use folders to organize my files?** You can store thousands of files on one storage device. Without folders, it would be difficult to find the file you want. You create folders to hold folders and files. Folders within folders are **nested folders**, also called **subfolders**. You give folders descriptive names to help you remember what is in the folders.

- **How do I know which folder to use?** As you'll recall, Windows supplies default folders. When you save a file, you can use a default folder, you can create a new folder at the same level as the default folder, or you can create subfolders in any folder. You create folders and subfolders to meet your needs. For example, you might create a subfolder named TownProject in the default My Documents folder to hold documents related to a project in town. Within that folder you might create another subfolder named Budgets for all the spreadsheets containing budget data.

- **How do I create new folders?** To create a new folder, you can use Windows Explorer. With Windows Explorer open, you can navigate to the location on the storage device where you want to create the folder. Once you have selected the drive and folder location for the new folder, you click the New Folder button on the menu bar to create a new folder. Then, when it is created, a text box appears to the right of the folder. You type the folder name in the text box. See Figure D-6. Be sure to give the folder a meaningful name that will help you remember what files are stored in that folder. File and folder naming rules restrict you from using special characters such as a colon or a slash in folder names. Filenaming conventions are discussed in the next lesson.

- **Can I copy or move a folder?** In addition to finding folders, Windows Explorer provides a set of file management tools that help you organize your folders. To work with a folder, you must select it. See Figure D-7. Once a folder is selected, you can copy, move, rename, or delete it as needed.

FIGURE D-6: Creating a new folder

TownProject folder is in My Documents folder | New folder button | Type to name the new folder

Used with permission from Microsoft

FIGURE D-7: Moving a folder

Target location | Folder being moved

Used with permission from Microsoft

- **Can I copy or move more than one folder at a time?** Yes, if you want to copy or move more than one folder, you can select more than one folder and then perform the action. To select more than one folder, you press and hold the Ctrl key while you click each folder you want to copy or move. Once selected, you can work with the selected folders just as you would work with a single folder. If the folders are right next to each other in the list, you can click the first folder, hold the Shift key, and then click the last folder in the list to select the first folder, the last folder, and all the folders between the two selected folders. You can also use the Ctrl key or the Shift key to work with more than one file.

- **What are folder properties?** Folder properties include the size of the folder, the date it was created, the number of files and folders contained in the folder, and the location or path to the folder. Folder properties also carry security and sharing information to determine who can access the folder and whether or not they can make changes to the folder.

- **Is there a way to see or change folder properties?** Windows Explorer lets you work with a folder's properties. With Windows Explorer open, you can right-click any folder, and then click Properties to open the Properties dialog box for the selected folder. See Figure D-8. For example, the

General tab in the Properties dialog box provides general information about the files and folders that are stored in that folder. Each tab in the Properties dialog box includes additional information about the selected folder. You will see different tabs depending on the location and properties of the selected folder.

- **What are folder options?** When you work with folders you have options for how you can open and view the folders. These options are features of the operating system that can be customized to meet your needs. For example, you can see different icons depending on the contents of a folder. You can also decide if you have to double or single click to open a folder.

- **How do I change folder options?** Sometimes you might want to change the way you view and search for files and folders in Windows Explorer. For example, you might want to display file icons representing file types in a folder as folder thumbnails. You may also choose to include hidden files and folders in a search of the folder. To view or change a folder's options, open the Folder Options dialog box. To open the Folder Options dialog box, you open the Control Panel, click Appearance and Personalization, and then click the Folders Option. In the Folders Option dialog box, you select one of the three tabs, General, View, and Search. Refer to Figure D-9 to see the General tab options.

FIGURE D-8: Properties dialog box for My Documents folder

Used with permission from Microsoft

FIGURE D-9: Folder Options dialog box

Used with permission from Microsoft

Folders and subfolders vs. directories and subdirectories

Directories and subdirectories mean the same thing as folders and subfolders when talking about file management. The operating system on your computer maintains a list of files called a **directory**. There is a directory for each storage device. The main directory of a drive is referred to as the **root directory**. On a PC, the root directory is typically identified by the device letter followed by a backslash. For example, the root directory of the hard drive would be C:\. A root directory is often subdivided into smaller **subdirectories**. When you use Windows, Mac OS, or a Linux graphical file manager, these subdirectories are depicted using icons that look like folders because subdirectories work like the folders in a filing cabinet to store related files.

Computer File Basics

There are several important elements that define a computer file. These include the contents of the file, the software that was used to create it, and the way the computer uses it. There are several categories of files, such as data files, executable files, configuration files, and drivers. Most of the files you create on your computer are data files. Although files can contain different data, they have several key elements, including filename, format, location, size, and date.

Learning Objective 3:
Identify the key elements of a computer file

- **What is a filename?** A **filename** is a set of letters, symbols, or numbers that identifies a file. A filename consists of a name followed by a period, followed by a file extension. Every saved file has a filename.

- **Are there rules I need to know for naming files?** Yes, the filename must follow specific rules, called **filenaming conventions**. Each operating system has a unique set of filenaming conventions. When you use the Windows operating system, you cannot use the symbols : * \ < > | " / and ? as part of a filename. If you try to save the file using one of the restricted symbols, you will receive a message telling you there is a problem with the filename. When you name a file, you should give it a meaningful name that can help you remember the contents of the file.

- **What are file extensions?** A **file extension** (or **filename extension**) is a set of letters and/or numbers added to the end of filename following a period that helps to identify the file contents or file type. A file extension helps describes the file contents. For example, the music files you listen to on your portable media player probably have the .mp3 file extension. A file extension is separated from the main filename by a period, as in BornToRun.mp3. In this example, the file extension .mp3 indicates that this is a music file.

  You will also recognize that some file extensions are associated with a particular application program. See Table D-1 for a list of some common file extensions. Knowing the file extension can help you identify which application program was used to create the data file. Once you know the file format, you will know which application to use if you want to open the file. A software program can typically open a file that exists in its **native file format**, plus several additional **file formats**.

TABLE D-1: Common file extensions

File extensions	Application
xls, xlsx	Microsoft Excel
doc, docx	Microsoft Word
txt, rtf	Text editor (WordPad, Notepad)
ppt, pptx	Microsoft PowerPoint
mdb, accdb	Microsoft Access
gif, tif, jpg, bmp, raw, png	Graphic or photo viewer or editor
wav, mid, mp3	Music and sound player or editor
zip	Compressed file
pdf	Adobe Acrobat or Reader

© Cengage Learning

As you work with files, you will begin to recognize that some file extensions, such as .txt (text file) or .jpg (graphics file), indicate a file type (such as a document or a photograph). They are not specific to any one program. Understanding file extensions can help you if you receive a file but they don't tell you much about the file's contents.

- **Do I decide the file extensions?** Generally, no. As a user, you do not decide the extension. The software program assigns an extension to the file automatically when you save it. Some programs give you several options. For example, when you save a graphic you can decide if you want a jpg, tif, or some other graphic format.

- **Can I change the file extension?** Technically, yes, but you really shouldn't change file extensions because a file extension is usually related to the file format. Sometimes, a file extension is changed in error when you try to rename a file. Be careful to change only the name to the left of the period when you change a filename. If you change a file extension while renaming a file, the file will not be able to be opened.

● **Why can't I see the file extensions when I look at my files using Windows Explorer?** File extensions should be shown by default. If you can't see the file extensions, you can change the settings to show them. It is a good idea to show file extensions because they help you know the file type. To view file extensions, be sure the Hide extensions for known file types check box in the Folder Options dialog box does not have a check mark.

● **When do I name a file?** You name a file the first time you save it. You can rename a file any time after it has been saved. One way, you can rename a file is to use the Save As command.

● **How do I know when to use Save and when to use Save As?** The flowchart in Figure D-10 can help you decide whether to use the Save or the Save As command. When you try to use the Save command for a file that has not been saved, the program will open the Save As dialog box, even though you selected the Save command.

FIGURE D-10: Save or Save As?

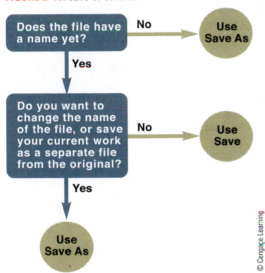

© Cengage Learning

● **Why can't I open some files?** If you can't open file, you might see a warning message like the one shown in Figure D-11.

FIGURE D-11: Unrecognized file type

Used with permission from Microsoft

You might not be able to open a file for one of the following reasons:

- You do not have the software application needed to open the file.
- The file might have been damaged—or corrupted—by a transmission or disk error.
- The file extension might have been changed, perhaps while renaming the file, and so the file is no longer associated with its application program. In this situation, if you think you know the correct file extension, you can change the file extension again and try to open the file.
- The file might use a file format for a newer version of the software than you have. For example, Office 2010 files use a new file format that is not able to be opened by Office 2003 programs unless you have a special compatibility program.

Several Web sites provide lists of file extensions and their corresponding software. By looking up a file extension in one of these lists, you can find out what application software you'll need to open a file based on its file extension.

● **What other information is stored with each of my files?** The File Properties dialog box is a good way to find out information about a file. See Figure D-12. General information such as file size and file date can be helpful as you manage your files. **File size** is usually measured in bytes, kilobytes, or megabytes. Knowing the size of a file can be important, especially when you are sending a file as an email attachment. Your computer's operating system keeps track of file sizes. Your computer also keeps track of the date on which a file was created or last modified. The **file date** is useful if you have saved a file using slightly different filenames each time and you want to know which is the most recent.

FIGURE D-12: File Properties dialog box for Kalimba.mp3

Used with permission from Microsoft

How to Manage Computer Files

To manage files, you use the same file management tools you used to copy, move, rename, or delete a folder. As you work with programs, you will need to open and save files. You can open files while working with an application program or by using a file management program. You can also save files from within an application program such as a word processor.

Learning Objective 4:
Describe the file management steps for working with files

● **Do I have to remember all the information about where my files are stored?** No, you don't have to remember the details, but it is helpful to create a system for naming files and folders that is easy for you to use. Although file management programs, like Windows Explorer, help you locate your files, knowing the basics (the drive, the folder name(s), and the filename) will help you find your files faster.

Most application software provides access to file management tasks through the Save, Save As, and Open dialog boxes. Table D-2 lists additional file management tasks you will use when working with files and folders.

TABLE D-2: Additional file management tasks

File or folder command	Description and examples
Rename	Change the name of a file or folder to describe its contents better. For example, you might change the name of the file Letter.docx to Letter to Pam 10-6.docx. When renaming a file, be careful to keep the same file extension so that you can open it with the correct application software.
Copy	Create a copy of a file or folder; the file remains in the original location and a duplicate file is added to a different location. For example, copy a document file to a new folder so that you can revise the content in the copy and leave the original content intact.
Move	Move a file or folder from one folder to another, or from one storage device to another. For example, move a file to a new folder to organize your hard drive. When you move a file or folder, it is erased from its original location.
Delete	Remove the file from the folder and place it in the Recycle Bin. For example, delete a file or folder with files when you no longer need it. Note: most file management programs delete all the files (and subfolders) in a folder when you delete a folder.

● **What is a file tag?** Some applications also allow you to add tags to a file. A **file tag** is a short word or phrase that describes a file. It is useful when you search for a file. Tags appear in the Details pane in Windows Explorer, see Figure D-13, as well as on the Details tab of the Properties dialog box. For example, tags help you describe the location, camera settings, and people pictured in a photograph.

FIGURE D-13: Tags provide additional information about a file

Selected file not yet tagged   Current tags

● **Is it possible to convert a file from one format to another?** Yes. The easiest way to convert a file from one format to another is to find an application program that works with both file formats. Graphics programs can often handle most of the major file formats for graphics. For example, you can use a program such as Paint to convert a graphics file from the .tif file format to the .bmp file format. To do this, open the file using the Paint program. Once the file is open, click the File tab, then click the Save As command to see other possible formats. If you have a specific need for a format not listed, click Other formats to open the Save As dialog box. You then select a new file format, assign the file a new name if you want, and save it. See Figure D-14.

Used with permission from Microsoft

● **Are there rules and guidelines I should follow when managing files?** Yes. The following tips will help you manage your files:

- Use descriptive names. Give your files and folders descriptive names when you save or create them, and avoid using cryptic abbreviations.

- Maintain file extensions. When renaming a file, keep the original file extension so that you can open it with the correct application software.

- Group similar files and consider using the default folders in Windows, such as Documents, Pictures, Music, and so on. Separate files into folders based on subject matter. For example, store your creative writing assignments in one appropriately named folder and your music files in another appropriately named folder.

- Do not mix data files and program files, that is, do not store data files in the folders that hold your software. On computers running Windows, most software programs are stored in subfolders of the Program Files folder.

- Do not store programs or data files in the root directory (C:\) of your computer's hard drive. It is better to create folders and store your files in those folders.

- Be aware of storage locations. When you save files, make sure the drive letter and folder name specify the correct storage location.

- Organize your folders from the top down. When creating a hierarchy of folders, consider how you want to access and back up files. A **backup** is a copy of your files made for safekeeping. You should back up your folders regularly. For example, it your files are stored in one folder, such as the My Documents folder, then it is easy to backup that folder and all nested subfolders. If your important data is scattered in a variety of folders, however, making backups is more time consuming.

- Access files from the hard drive. For best performance, copy files from portable storage media to your computer's hard drive before accessing them.

- Follow copyright rules. When copying files, make sure you do not violate copyright and license restrictions.

- Delete or archive files you no longer need. Deleting unneeded files and folders helps keep your list of files from growing to an unmanageable size. One way to delete a file is to right-click the file name in Windows Explorer, and the click Delete on the shortcut menu. File archiving utility programs combine a number of files together into one archive file, or a series of archive files, for long-term storage.

Deleting folders and files

The Windows Recycle Bin and similar utilities in other operating systems protect you from accidentally deleting folders and files from your hard drive. When you give the command to delete a folder or file, the operating system moves the folder or file to the Recycle Bin folder. See Figure D-15. The deleted folder or file still takes up space on the hard drive, but it does not appear in the usual directory listing. The folder file does, however, appear in the directory listing for the Recycle Bin folder. You can undelete any folders or files in this listing. It is important to remember that only folders or files you delete from your hard drive are sent to the Recycle Bin. Folders or files you delete from a removable storage medium, such as a USB device, CD, or DVD, are not sent to the Recycle Bin.

FIGURE D-15: Recycle Bin empty and full

Used with permission from Microsoft

Bin empty   Bin full

How Computers Represent Data

Data representation refers to the way in which data is created, stored, processed, output, and transmitted. It is the technology that makes it possible for you to use digital electronic devices such as iPods, GPS devices, mobile phones, and computers. Data representation makes it possible to input, store, process, and display text, numbers, graphics, photos, or play music and videos. Digital data is represented using the binary number system.

Learning Objective 5:
Describe how digital data representation produces numbers, text, images, video, and sound

● **What is the binary number system?** The **binary number system** makes it possible for computers to represent data simply by using 0s and 1s. The 0s and 1s are translated into electrical on and off signals that the computer can understand.

Table D-3 compares the decimal number system with the binary number system. Notice that the decimal system, base 10, uses ten symbols (0, 1, 2, 3, 4, 5, 6, 7, 8, and 9) to represent numbers. The binary number system has only two digits: 0 and 1.

TABLE D-3: Comparing the decimal and binary number systems

Decimal	Binary	Decimal	Binary
0	0	7	111
1	1	8	1000
2	10	9	1001
3	11	10	1010
4	100	11	1011
5	101	1000	1111101000
6	110	1001	1111101001

© Cengage Learning

● **What is digital data?** **Digital data** is text, numbers, graphics, sound, and video that has been converted into the digits 0 and 1. All digital data is created from 0s and 1s. The 0s and 1s are electronic signals that represent on and off, or yes and no, respectively. The computer interprets these electronic signals as data.

● **How does the computer interpret these electronic signals?** The electronic signals are coded as a series of 0s and 1s. Each 0 or 1 is one **binary digit**, or **bit**. A series of eight bits is referred to as a **byte**. Each byte represents one piece of data, such as the letter g, the number 5, or one dot

in a picture. Bytes are coded using different coding schemes. Most computer coding schemes use eight bits to represent each number, letter, or symbol.

Digital computers use many different coding schemes to represent data. The coding scheme used by a computer depends on whether the data is numeric or character data. **Numeric data** includes numbers that might be used in arithmetic operations such as your annual income, your age, or the cost of dinner.

● **How can my computer process character data?** **Character data** is composed of letters, symbols, and numerals that will not be used in arithmetic operations. Examples of character data include your name, address, and telephone number. Character data is represented by coding schemes, which use a series of 1s and 0s. For example, when you type the word dog, you press the key that represents each letter. As you press each key, an electronic signal is sent to the processor. The signal is the code for the letter you typed. See Figure D-16.

FIGURE D-16: Coding data

01100111

dog

The letter g as digital code

© Cengage Learning

The most common coding schemes for coding character data are ASCII, EBCDIC, and Unicode. Unicode is the most flexible, and currently provides code for characters from all written languages, including languages such as Chinese, Russian, and Hebrew. Modern personal computers use the Extended ASCII (American Standard Code for Information Interchange) coding scheme.

- **How can my computer process numbers to be used in calculations?** Computers use the binary number system to represent numeric data. So, when you type the number you want to use in a calculation, such as 3, the number is converted to its binary representation, 11. The computer recognizes this digital data as the number 3.

- **How can my computer process images, such as the photos from my camera?** Images, such as photos, pictures, line art, and graphs, are not discrete objects like a number or letter of the alphabet. A computer must **digitize** the information that makes up the picture (such as the colors) into 1s and 0s. Digitized images are a series of colored dots, also called **pixels** (picture elements). See Figure D-17. Each pixel is assigned a binary number based on the color of that pixel. A digital image is simply a list of binary numbers for all the dots it contains. Each binary number in the list is associated with one pixel. The computer interprets the list of numbers to recreate the image.

FIGURE D-17: Pixels in an image

© Cengage Learning

Each pixel is assigned a binary number based on its color.

- **How are digital sound files created?** Sounds are continuous analog sound waves. In order for a computer to understand a sound, it must digitize the information that makes up the sound. Sound, such as music and speech, is characterized by the properties of a sound wave. An analog sound wave is digitized by sampling it at various points, and then converting those points into digital numbers. The more samples your computer takes, the closer the points come to approximating the full wave pattern. This process of sampling, as shown in Figure D-18, is how digital recordings, such as the music files on your portable media player, are made.

FIGURE D-18: Digitizing sound

An analog sound wave is a smooth curve of continous values.

To digitize a wave, it is sliced into vertical segments, called samples.

© Cengage Learning

More about bits and bytes

As discussed, a bit is one binary digit, and a byte is eight bits. The word bit can be abbreviated as a lowercase b, and the word byte can be abbreviated as an uppercase B. The terms used to quantify computer data are summarized in Table D-4. The prefixes **kilo-** (thousands), **mega-** (millions), **giga-** (billions), **tera-** (trillion), **peta-** (thousand trillion), **exa-** (quintillion), and **zetta-** (sextillion) are used for large amounts of data.

Bits and bytes are used in different ways. Data transmission speeds are usually expressed in bits, whereas storage space is usually expressed in bytes. Typically, kilobytes (KB) are used to refer to most common documents, megabytes (MB) are used to refer to RAM, and gigabytes (GB) are used to refer to hard drive, optical storage media, and solid-state drive capacities. In an iPod ad, you might notice that it can store up to 160 GB or 160 gigabytes of music and video. The Internet data transfer speed for your computer might be listed as 5 Mbps or 5 megabits per second.

TABLE D-4: Terms used to describe digital data

Term	Value	Term	Value
Bit	1 binary digit	**Byte**	8 bits
Kilobit (Kb)	1,000 bits (exactly 1,024)	**Kilobyte (KB)**	1,000 bytes (exactly 1,024)
Megabit (Mb)	1 million bits	**Megabyte (MB)**	1 million bytes
Gigabit (Gb)	1 billion bits	**Gigabyte (GB)**	1 billion bytes
Terabyte (TB)	1 trillion bytes	**Petabyte (PB)**	1,000 terabytes (2^{50} bytes)
Exabyte (EB)	1,000 petabytes (2^{60} bytes)	**Zettabyte (ZB)**	1,000 exabytes (2^{70} bytes)

© Cengage Learning

(Note: All values are approximate unless noted otherwise.)

Integrated Circuits— An Overview

Computers and digital devices are electronic devices that use electrical signals to process data. The electronic parts of a personal computer store, process, and transfer the data. In the beginning, the electronic parts were large and bulky. Over time, the electronic parts have become smaller and more efficient. The most significant technology that made the miniaturization of electronics parts possible is the integrated circuit.

Learning Objective 6:
Define integrated circuits and explain the role they play inside a computer

● **What is an integrated circuit?** An **integrated circuit (IC)** is a very thin slice of semiconducting material, such as silicon and germanium. ICs are packed with microscopic circuit elements. See Figure D-19. These elements include wires, transistors, capacitors, logic gates, and resistors, and are used to create miniature electronic parts and pathways. Electronic signals, the bits and bytes, travel over these electronic pathways. The terms **computer chip**, microchip, and **chip** are all synonymous with the term integrated circuit. Chips are manufactured in sterile environments to protect their parts.

FIGURE D-19: An integrated circuit

Courtesy of Intel Corporation; © Wetchawut/Shutterstock.com

● **Are there chips in all electronic devices?** Yes, chips are not only in a computer's system unit but also in other electronic devices, such as tablet computers, smartphones, and GPS devices. Chips are also embedded in appliances such as refrigerators, microwaves, and cars. In fact, electronic devices use integrated circuits for processors, memory, and support circuitry.

● **What protects chips from possibly being damaged?** Each chip is packaged in a protective carrier or chip package. Chip packages vary in shape and size. The **DIP (dual inline package)** chip package is small with caterpillar-like legs protruding from a black, rectangular body. The **PGA (pin-grid array)** chip package resembles a pincushion. The **DIMM (dual inline memory module)** chip package is long and slim. See Figure D-20.

FIGURE D-20: Packaging for integrated circuits

A DIP chip package

A DIMM chip package

A PGA chip package

© Arber/Shutterstock.com; Courtesy of MediaTechnics Corporation; © Richard Lister/Shutterstock.com

● **How are all these chip packages connected to the computer?** Chip packages are connected to the computer's motherboard. As you'll recall from Unit A, the **motherboard** is the computer's main circuit board. See Figure D-21. The DIP and PGA chip packages are plugged into sockets and connectors on the motherboard. DIMM chip packages and small circuit boards are plugged into slots on the motherboard. Some chips are soldered permanently in place. The motherboard contains the electronic circuitry that connects all these parts. As discussed in Unit B, expansion cards attach to the motherboard through expansion slots.

Because some chips can be inserted and removed easily, they can be replaced if they become damaged or need to be upgraded. Sometimes, multiple chips are required for a single function, such as generating stereo-quality sound. In this case, the chips might be housed on a separate small circuit board, such as an expansion card.

FIGURE D-21: Chips on a motherboard

Adapter card with chips   Memory using a DIMM chip package   CPU using a PGA chip package

● **What is a processor?** A **processor** (also called a **microprocessor**) is one type of chip or integrated circuit. The main processor in a personal computer is the **CPU (central processing unit).** It is designed to process instructions. A processor is a very complex integrated circuit, containing hundreds of millions of miniaturized electronic parts. See Figure D-22. It is the most important and usually the most expensive single part of a computer. Looking inside a computer, you can usually identify the processor because it is the largest chip on the motherboard. Most of today's processors are housed in a PGA chip

FIGURE D-22: Every digital device has a processor

Desktop processor   Smartphone processor

package. All digital devices have processors. As you might suspect, processors for mobile devices such as smartphones, cameras, and tablet computers are smaller than processors for desktop computers.

● **Which companies produce most of today's popular PC processors?** Intel is the world's largest chipmaker and supplies a sizeable percentage of the processors that power PCs. AMD (Advanced Micro Devices) is Intel's chief rival in the PC chip market. It produces processors that work just like Intel's chips but at a lower price. Processors for mobile devices are also made by companies such as ARM, Texas Instruments, Samsung, and NVIDIA.

A typical personal computer ad contains a long list of specifications describing a computer's parts and technical details. Most computer specifications begin with the processor brand, type, and speed. The processors that are marketed with today's computers will handle most business, educational, and entertainment applications.

● **How can I tell what CPU my computer uses?** You can use software to identify your computer's CPU and its specifications. If you are running Windows, you can access this information through the Windows Control Panel. See Figure D-23. If you have a Mac, click About This Mac from the Apple menu in the upper-left menu bar, and then click More Info to view the name of the processor.

FIGURE D-23: Installed processor specs

Used with permission from Microsoft

● **Can I replace my computer's processor with a faster or better one?** Yes, it is possible to upgrade your computer's processor, but computer owners rarely do. The price of the latest, greatest processor can often get you more than halfway to buying an entirely new computer system. Technical factors also discourage processor upgrades. A processor operates at full efficiency only if all parts in the computer can handle the faster speeds.

Processors—An Overview

As discussed in the previous lesson, the central processing unit (CPU) contains all the circuitry that performs the central processing tasks of the computer on a single chip. Different personal computers come with different processors. Processors have certain factors in common. Knowing how each of the processor's factors affects the performance of a computer can help you can make an informed decision when buying a computer.

Learning Objective 7:
Explain how CPU factors affect computer performance

● **What factors affect processor performance?** A processor's performance is affected by several factors, including number of cores, clock speed, bus speed, word size, and cache memory size. These factors combine to affect the processing speed, which determines the computer's performance. A processor's factors are described as part of a processor's specs (also called specifications). A processor's specs are available on its processor manufacturer's Web site and in processor documentation. You can also access this information about your computer through third-party software, such as CPU-Z. See Figure D-24.

FIGURE D-24: Specs for a processor using the CPU-Z program

● **What do processor specs tell me about the processor?** Computer ads typically include specs that determine a processor's performance. Figure D-25 shows

the specs for an Intel Core i7 quad-core processor in part of a sample computer ad. A processor that contains circuitry for more than one processing unit on a single chip is called a **multi-core processor**. Multi-core processors (such as dual-core and quad-core processors) are faster than processors with a single core. To gain maximum speed, however, your computer's operating system and software should be optimized for multi-core processing. Most operating systems support multi-core processing.

FIGURE D-25: Processor specs in an ad

Intel Core i7 2860QM processor 2.50 GHz 1600 MHz FSB 8 MB L2 cache

© Cengage Learning

● **What is clock speed?** The **processor clock** is a timing device that sets the pace (the clock speed) for executing instructions. The **clock speed** is specified in megahertz (MHz), which is millions of cycles per second, or gigahertz (GHz), which is billions of cycles per second. A **cycle** is the smallest unit of time a processor can recognize. The faster the clock, the more instructions the processor can execute per second. For the processor in the sample ad shown in Figure D-26, the clock speed is 2.50 GHz. This means the processor's clock operates at 2.5 billion cycles per second.

FIGURE D-26: Clock speed specs in an ad

Intel Core i7 2860QM processor 2.50 GHz 1600 MHz FSB 8 MB L2 cache

© Cengage Learning

● **What is bus speed?** A **bus** is an electronic pathway that carries the electronic signals between the electronic parts of a computer. Bus speed identifies how fast the electronic signals move along the bus pathway. **FSB** stands for **front side bus**.

This term refers to the circuitry that transports data to and from the processor. See Figure D-27.

Currently, FSB speed is measured in megahertz (MHz). In the sample ad in Figure D-28, the FSB speed is 1600 MHz. When comparing processors, larger numbers indicate faster FSB speeds.

FIGURE D-27: Front side bus

Wires transfer bits of information between the CPU and devices

Courtesy of Intel Corporation; © Cengage Learning; Courtesy of MediaTechnics Corporation

FIGURE D-28: Bus specs in an ad

Intel Core i7 2860QM processor 2.50 GHz 1600 MHz FSB 8 MB L2 cache

© Cengage Learning

● **What is word size?** Word size refers to the number of bits that a processor can manipulate at one time. A processor with a 32-bit word size, for example, has 32-bit registers, processes 32 bits at one time, and is referred to as a 32-bit processor. Processors with a larger word size can process more data during each processor cycle. Today's personal computers typically contain 32-bit or 64-bit processors.

● **What is cache?** Cache, also called RAM cache or cache memory, is high-speed memory that a processor can access more rapidly than memory elsewhere on the motherboard. The amount of cache memory, as well as its location, affects performance. A Level 1 (L1) cache is built into the processor chip, whereas a Level 2 (L2) cache is located on a separate chip, and so it takes a processor more time to get data from the L2 cache to the processor. Usually, cache capacity is expressed in megabytes (MB). The processor in the sample ad in Figure D-29 has 8 MB L2 cache.

FIGURE D-29: Cache specs in an ad

Intel Core i7 2860QM processor 2.50 GHz 1600 MHz FSB 8 MB L2 cache

© Cengage Learning

● **How can I tell which processor best meets my needs?** You can use benchmark results to compare the results to other processors. Benchmarking is a technique used across many industries to compare and measure performance. Testing laboratories run a series of tests called benchmarks to gauge the overall speed of a processor. The results of benchmark tests are usually available on the Web and are published in computer magazine articles.

All things being equal, a computer with a 3.8 GHz processor is faster than a computer with a 2.4 GHz processor—and a computer with a processor that has a larger word size can process more data during each processor cycle than a computer with a processor that has a smaller word size. Furthermore, all things being equal, a computer with Level 1 cache is faster than a computer with the same amount of Level 2 cache. But all things are not equal so you can use benchmark test results to compare processors before you buy a computer.

● **Is there a way for me to find out how my computer measures up?** Windows 7 offers a set of benchmarks called the Windows Experience Index. This index scores a computer's overall performance, as well as the performance of components such as its processor, memory, graphics, and storage system. You can see this on your Windows computer through the Performance Tools section of the Control Panel. See Figure D-30.

FIGURE D-30: Windows Experience Score

Used with permission from Microsoft

Subscores help you gauge performance for individual components

The base score provides an overall performance benchmark

How the processor gets instructions

Computer programmers write programs that control computers. These programs include the instructions that tell a processor what to do. These programs are usually written in a high-level programming language. The human-readable version of a program is called source code. Source code has to be converted into a digital format before the processor can use it. The procedure for translating source code into 0s and 1s is done by a compiler or an interpreter. A compiler converts all the statements in a program in a single batch. The resulting collection of instructions, called object code, is placed in a new file. Most of the program files distributed as software contain object code that is ready for the processor to execute. An interpreter converts and executes one statement at a time while the program is running.

Computer Memory: RAM

Memory is the electronic circuitry that holds data and instructions so it is available when needed by a computer. Computers use four categories of memory: random access memory (RAM), virtual memory, read-only memory (ROM), and EEPROM memory. Each type of memory is characterized by the type of data it contains and the technology it uses to hold the data. This lesson discusses random access memory, commonly called RAM.

Learning Objective 8:
Define RAM and explain its importance to computers

● **What is RAM?** In a personal computer, **RAM (random access memory)** is the waiting room for the computer's processor. RAM is usually several chips or small circuit boards that plug into the motherboard. RAM holds operating system instructions that control the basic functions of a computer system. These instructions are loaded into RAM every time you start your computer. These instructions are stored in RAM until you turn off your computer. RAM is also a temporary holding area for program instructions, as well as for data waiting to be processed, displayed, or printed. In addition, RAM holds the results of processing until they can be stored more permanently using a storage system. Refer to Figure D-31.

FIGURE D-31: RAM is a a temporary holding area

Courtesy of MediaTechnics Corporation; Used with permission from Microsoft

● **Does RAM matter?** Yes. The amount of RAM your computer has makes a difference in how well your computer can perform. Usually the more RAM your computer has, the better the performance. In fact, along with processor speed, RAM capacity is the other most important factor in determining and comparing the power of a computer system. The performance of your computer is directly related to how much RAM is available for your applications, data, and operating system. RAM is made by different manufacturers. Be

sure to read reviews about a RAM product before purchasing it because quality can affect performance.

● **How does RAM work?** In RAM, electronic parts called **capacitors** hold the bits that represent data. You can visualize the capacitors as microscopic lights that can be turned on or off. A charged capacitor is turned on and represents a 1 bit. A discharged capacitor is turned off and represents a 0 bit. You can visualize the capacitors as being arranged in banks of eight. Refer to Figure D-32. Each bank holds eight bits, or one byte, of data. Each RAM location has an address and holds one byte of data. A RAM address at each location helps the computer locate data as needed for processing. The content of RAM is changed by changing the charge of each capacitor. The capacitor charge is changed when you input data and the computer processes that data.

FIGURE D-32: How RAM works

© Cengage Learning

The two charged capacitors at this RAM address represent the letter A.

A different sequence of charged capacitors represents the letter B.

Another sequence of charged capacitors represents the letter C.

● **How does RAM differ from hard drive storage on my computer?** RAM holds data temporarily in circuitry that's directly connected to the motherboard. In contrast, the hard drive stores data on magnetic or solid-state media. Data in RAM is temporary storage. Data stored on the hard drive storage is more permanent. In some respects, RAM is similar to a whiteboard. You can use a whiteboard to write formulas, erase them, and then write an outline for a report. In a similar way,

RAM can hold the numbers and formulas you need when you use spreadsheet software to balance your checkbook, and RAM can hold the text of your English essay when you use word processing software. Unlike a whiteboard, however, RAM is volatile, which means that it requires electrical power to hold data. If the computer is turned off or if the power goes out, all data in RAM instantly and permanently disappears.

● **How much RAM should my personal computer have?** The amount of RAM your computer needs depends on the software that you use. The capacity of RAM is expressed either in megabytes (MB) or gigabytes (GB). Today's personal computers typically feature 2–8 GB of RAM. If you are using a Windows computer, you can view information about your computer, including how much RAM is currently installed, using the Control Panel. See Figure D-33.

FIGURE D-33: Installed RAM specs

RAM requirements are routinely specified on the outside of a software package. If you want to buy a new program that needs more RAM than is installed on your computer, you can purchase and install additional RAM. However, the amount of RAM is limited by the computer's motherboard, such as by the number of slots the motherboard has to hold RAM. The manufacturer of the motherboard sets the limits. Also, if you plan to upgrade, contact the manufacturer of the computer or motherboard so you can be sure to buy the correct type of RAM.

● **Why is it important to have the most RAM possible?** RAM capacity makes a difference you can notice. For example, if you are working on a spreadsheet, the program instructions and the worksheet are stored in RAM. See Figure D-34. With lots of RAM, you will notice that calculations happen faster and that many graphics operations take less time than with a computer that has less RAM capacity.

FIGURE D-34: RAM influences performance

● **Does RAM speed make a difference?** Yes. The amount of time that RAM takes to write or to read data once the request has been received from the processor is called the access time. So, faster RAM generally means faster performance. RAM speed is often expressed in **nanoseconds (ns)**, which are billionths of a second. Whenever referring to nanoseconds, lower numbers mean faster transmission and processing of data. For example, 8 ns RAM is faster than 10 ns RAM. RAM speed can also be expressed in MHz (millions of cycles per second). This measurement is used so RAM speed can be compared to clock speed. The way you interpret MHz rates is just the opposite of the way you interpret nanosecond rates. Higher MHz ratings mean faster speeds. For example, 1066 MHz RAM is faster than 800 MHz RAM.

● **How can I know if the computer I want to buy has enough RAM?** Most computer ads specify RAM capacity, speed, and type. The ad also provides important information about the maximum amount of RAM that can be installed in the computer. For example, a computer ad might list the specifications shown in the partial ad in Figure D-35.

FIGURE D-35: RAM specs in an ad

2 GB Dual Channel DDR2 SDRAM at 1066 MHz (max 4 GB)

The specs in this ad mean the following: the computer currently has 2 gigabytes of installed RAM. The RAM uses dual-channel, double data rate 2 SDRAM. **SDRAM (Synchronous DRAM)** is a generic name for various kinds of DRAM that are synchronized with the clock speed for which the processor is optimized. Most of today's personal computers use SDRAM. Innovations such as dual-channel technology and double data rate (DDR, DDR2, or DDR3) have increased SDRAM speed. The ad indicates the RAM speed is measured at 1066 MHz. It also indicates that this computer can have a maximum 4 GB of RAM.

Other Types of Computer Memory

In addition to RAM, a computer uses other types of memory. Virtual memory, ROM, and EEPROM are the other main categories of memory commonly used in computers. This lesson looks at these types of computer memory and how all computer memory types work together.

Learning Objective 9:
Explain how a computer uses virtual memory, ROM, and EEPROM

● **What is virtual memory?** Although, technically, RAM cannot be full, it can reach near capacity. If you open several application programs and several large graphics or videos at the same time, you can push RAM to its limit. When this occurs, the computer slows down. You might notice that it takes longer to load a screen or respond to a command. To help solve this problem, the operating system uses an area of the hard drive to temporarily store data from RAM. This area of the hard drive is called **virtual memory**. The data that has been moved from RAM to virtual memory is called a **swap file**. See Figure D-36. Virtual memory stores parts of a program or data file until needed. By exchanging the data in RAM with the data in virtual memory, your computer gains almost unlimited memory capacity.

FIGURE D-36: How virtual memory works

Data is copied from RAM to the virtual memory area of the hard drive and back again as needed for processing.

RAM

Hard drive

Courtesy of MediaTechnics Corporation

Too much dependence on virtual memory can have a negative effect on your computer's performance. Getting data from a mechanical device, such as a hard drive, is much slower than getting data from an electronic device, such as RAM. Installing as much RAM as your computer system allows will help your computer improve its performance.

● **What is ROM?** **ROM (read-only memory)** is a type of memory that holds the computer's startup routine and other basic system information. ROM is housed in a single integrated circuit and is usually a large chip that is plugged into the motherboard. Unlike RAM, which is temporary and volatile, ROM is permanent and nonvolatile. The instructions in ROM are permanent and are not lost even when the computer power is turned off. The only way to change the instructions in ROM is to replace the ROM chip. To overcome this limitation, some newer computers use flash memory chips instead of ROM for storing the startup routine and other system information. Flash memory chips can be changed and they do not lose data when the power is turned off.

● **Does ROM control the boot process?** Yes. When you turn on a computer, the ROM circuitry receives power and begins the boot process by executing the bootstrap program. As discussed in Unit C, the boot process has six major events, including the power-on self-test (POST). See Figure D-37. During the boot process, the bootstrap program in ROM instructs the core operating system programs to load into RAM.

FIGURE D-37: POST screen

Péter Gudella/Shutterstock.com; © Cengage Learning

● **When I boot my computer, sometimes I see a message about BIOS. What is that?** When you turn on your computer, the processor receives electrical power and is ready to begin executing instructions. But, because the power was off, RAM is empty and contains no instructions for the processor to execute. Your computer needs to know how much memory is available so that it can allocate space for all of the programs that you want to run. This configuration information cannot be stored in RAM because no information is in RAM when the computer power is turned off. Instead, this configuration information is stored in ROM.

ROM contains a small set of instructions called the **ROM BIOS (basic input/output system)**. When the computer is turned on, the BIOS message tells you that the operating system is reading the configuration settings. While ROM BIOS instructions are accomplished mainly without user intervention, the computer will not function without the ROM chip and the BIOS instructions. You know the boot process is complete when the operating system is loaded into RAM and your computer is ready to accept commands. See Figure D-38.

FIGURE D-38: ROM and the boot process

Boot program tells hard drive to load the OS

Hard drive

ROM

OS kernel loaded into RAM

RAM

Operating system is available as needed.

Processor

Courtesy of MediaTechnics Corporation

● **How does the computer recognize the devices connected to my computer?** When you turn on your computer, the boot program checks the configuration settings to see what hardware and which devices are connected to your computer. When you add new hardware, the computer needs information about the hardware in order to recognize the hardware you added. This information is stored in the configurations settings. Computer configuration settings include the date and time, hard drive capacity, number of CD/DVD/BD drives, and RAM capacity.

● **Are the configurations stored in ROM?** No. Remember that ROM holds data on a permanent basis. It cannot be used to store configuration settings because the data in ROM cannot be updated when new hardware is added. For example, if you add more memory modules, the computer could not update the memory specification information in ROM. This means the new memory would not be recognized by your computer system during the boot process. In order to be able to store and update basic system information, including configuration settings, your computer needs a type of memory that is more permanent than RAM but less permanent than ROM.

● **Where are configuration settings stored?** The configuration settings are stored in EEPROM. **EEPROM (electrically erasable programmable read-only memory)** is a nonvolatile chip that requires no power to hold data. So, when you change the configuration of your computer system—by adding RAM, for example—the data in EEPROM is updated. See Figure D-39.

FIGURE D-39: Configuration settings

Courtesy of Rachel B. Bunin

Some operating systems recognize such changes and automatically perform the update. If this does not happen, you can manually change EEPROM settings by running your computer's setup program. To access the EEPROM setup program on a Windows computer, hold down the F1 key as your computer boots. But be careful! If you make a mistake with these settings your computer might not be able to start.

Talking Points: Is Your Computer Making You Sick?

More and more workers spend their entire eight-hour day in front of a computer screen. Many work longer than the typical 40-hour workweek of eight-hour days for five days a week. Road warriors are lugging notebook computers through airports and trying to get work done in the cramped confines of economy seats. As computers and other digital devices continue to infiltrate the workplace, worker advocates are concerned about health risks associated with computer use. They raise questions about how the use of digital devices affect ordinary consumers, too. The general population in most developed countries own more digital gadgets and spend more time using them than ever before. Studies have shown that the average American spends about two hours a day using a computer. The popularity of LAN parties has spawned intensive daylong competitions, and many serious gamers are still hunched over their keyboards in the wee hours of the morning. It is rare to go anywhere and not see someone talking on a cell phone or plugged into a portable music player. How does this digital lifestyle affect the health of our nation and world?

Radiation Risks

Although we tend to associate radiation with the fallout from nuclear blasts and debilitating cancer treatments, the term refers simply to any energy that is emitted in the form of waves or particles. Radiation streams out of the sun in the form of heat and out of your stereo system as sound waves. Even more radiation pulses out from electrical appliances, wireless networks, cell phone towers, and electrical power lines. Most of the radiation in your everyday world is considered safe, especially in moderation. A few types of radiation can be harmful. Gamma rays and X-rays, for example, contain enough electromagnetic energy to alter chemical reactions in the body and disrupt molecules in human tissue. Shielding against these types of radiation is an important safety factor.

Every electronic device emits some type of radiation; otherwise, they would not be functional. The light emitted by computer, mobile phone, smartphone, and portable music player screens is essential for their use. Cell phones emit sound waves so we can listen to the person at the other end of the connection. Wireless routers emit radio waves to carry data from one workstation to another. Although the radiation from most digital gadgets is considered harmless, researchers have raised concerns about radiation from cell phones and computer display devices.

> **"The available scientific evidence does not allow us to conclude that mobile phones are absolutely safe, or that they are unsafe."**
>
> *U.S. Food and Drug Administration (FDA)*

LCD, LED, and OLED display devices generate an image by illuminating a matrix of tiny lights. LCD, LED, and OLED technologies have no tubes, no electron sprays, and generate no X-rays. LCD and OLED devices do, however, emit low levels of radiation. Emission levels vary depending on manufacturer, brand, and model. Monitors that meet TCO or MPR standards have emission levels believed to be safe. Various devices designed to block radiation are on the market, but their effectiveness is questionable. Regardless of the type of display device you use, do not sit too close to it. Your exposure to radiation is reduced the farther away you sit from it.

A mobile phone is a radio transmitter and receiver. It emits RF (radio frequency) energy. High levels of RF energy can heat human tissue in much the same way a microwave oven heats food. Compared to a microwave oven, however, the amount of radiation emitted by a cell phone is miniscule. The amount of radiation emitted by a cell phone can be measured by its specific absorption rate (SAR). You can find the SAR level for your cell phone by entering its FCC ID number (look for it in the user manual) at www.fcc.gov/oet/ea/fccid/. See Figure D-40.

FIGURE D-40: Finding the SAR for a cell phone

www.fcc.gov

You can also find SAR information on the phone manufacturer's Web site. In addition, a quick Google search reveals that SAR levels for mobile phones are listed on several Web pages. You can use these sites to compare SAR levels for different phones.

The scientific community continues to study and debate the amount of RF radiation that should be considered safe for long-term use. A recent Swedish study found evidence that long-term, extensive cell phone use significantly increases the risk of developing a brain tumor. A contradictory study performed by the London-based Institute of Cancer Research and three British universities found that cell phone use does not increase the incidence of brain tumors in cell phone users. Research literature is full of similar conflicting studies. Even the U.S. Food and Drug Administration (FDA) admits, "The available scientific evidence does not allow us to conclude that mobile phones are absolutely safe, or that they are unsafe."

> " Most of the health risks associated with computer use are not caused by the equipment itself, but by how the equipment is set up and used. "

The easiest way to reduce your exposure to mobile phone radiation is to use a hands-free headset. Headsets offer the additional benefit of reducing your chance of becoming involved in a traffic accident. Today, many states require the use of headsets while driving, See Figure D-41.

FIGURE D-41: Use a headset for mobile phone calls

© iStockphoto/Ron Bailey

Repetitive Stress Injuries

Most of the health risks associated with computer use are not caused by the equipment itself, but by how the equipment is set up and used. Improper positioning of your keyboard and mouse can cause repetitive stress injuries to wrists, arms, neck, back, and shoulders. A repetitive stress injury is not a specific disease. Instead, it is a group of similar overuse disorders that affect the tendons, muscles, and nerves.

Symptoms include stiffness and minor pain in your hands, wrists, arms, or shoulders. See Figure D-42. Your symptoms might appear while you're working, or they might appear several hours or days later. With rest, these injuries tend to heal. Although there are some problems, such as carpal tunnel syndrome, that might require medical intervention.

FIGURE D-42: Carpal Tunnel syndrome

© Alexonline/Shutterstock.com

Your wrist contains eight carpal bones surrounding a large nerve that controls your thumb, index, and ring fingers. How you place your hands on the keyboard can affect the pressure on that nerve. See Figure D-43. Anything that compresses this nerve, such as arthritis or thickened tendons, can cause numbness, pain, or tingling in your fingers. This condition is called carpal tunnel syndrome. At one time it was generally accepted that keyboarding was a major cause of carpal tunnel syndrome. A recent Mayo Clinic study, however, concluded that keyboarding does not cause carpal tunnel syndrome. Although the study did find that keyboarding can make the condition worse.

FIGURE D-43: Place your fingers correctly on the keyboard

Courtesy of Emily Bunin

Most computer-related hand and arm injuries are repetitive stress injuries, which can be avoided by following ergonomic guidelines. Ergonomics is the study of safe and efficient environments, particularly working environments. Ergonomics provides guidelines for making work environments safer and healthier. In the United States, the Occupational Safety and Health Administration (OSHA) sets and enforces standards for the safety and health of American workers. Although a federal law to enforce ergonomic standards in the workplace was repealed in 2001, many states have regulations designed to protect workers from repetitive stress injuries. You can review current OSHA policy by visiting their Web site at http://www.osha.gov/SLTC/ergonomics/index.html.

> **"Most computer-related hand and arm injuries are repetitive stress injuries, which can be avoided by following ergonomic guidelines."**

To avoid future computer-related stress injuries, keep ergonomic principles in mind wherever you work. The key to avoiding uncomfortable stress injuries is in the placement and use of your keyboard, mouse, monitor, desk, and chair. Figure D-44 provides an overview of ergonomic workstation guidelines. Some specific tips for setting up your keyboard and mouse follow:

- Position the keyboard so that it is just above your lap and your elbows are able to extend past the 90-degree angle when you type.

- When shopping for a computer desk, make sure it has a keyboard tray. The tray should be adjustable if possible. Also, look for one with a small lip that reduces the distance between the tray and your thighs.

- Angle the keyboard so that your wrists are straight when typing.

- If you have a wrist rest, use it only when you are not typing. Resting your wrist or arm on a wrist rest while typing causes your wrist to be at an angle that is not efficient.

- Use a keyboard that fits the size of your hands and fingers. When you rest your fingers on the home keys (asdf and jkl;), there should be 1/8 to 1/4 inch of space between them. When you type, your fingers should not be cramped together or overextended.

- Make sure your mouse is positioned close by so that you don't have to reach for it.

- Keep the mouse at the same height as your keyboard to minimize arm movements.

- Use your mouse with a relaxed arm and wrist.

- When working at mouse-intensive activities, you should change mouse hands occasionally. You might also consider using an air mouse or trackball, each of which requires a different set of muscles.

FIGURE D-44: Place your fingers correctly on the keyboard

Top 1/3 of screen at or slightly below eye level

Monitor 18"–22" from body (arm's length)

Keyboard on slight negative tilt (back of keyboard lower than front)

Knee angle greater than 90 degrees with feet in front of you

Feet flat on the floor or on footrest

Mouse in plane or slightly above plane of keyboard

Lean back slightly with back supported from pelvis to shoulder blades

Elbow angle slightly more than 90 degrees

Thighs parallel to floor

Approximately 2"–3" of space between back of knee and chair

© Cengage Learning

Eye Strain

Studies have found links between computer use and eye problems. The most common symptoms are sore, tired, burning, or itching eyes; watery eyes; dry eyes; blurred or double vision; headaches; difficulty shifting focus between the screen display and printed documents; and increased sensitivity to light. For many computer users, eye problems can be avoided by proper monitor placement and adjustment.

> **Studies have found links between computer use and eye problems.**

To position your monitor correctly, sit back slightly in your chair and stretch your right arm out straight ahead of you. Your middle finger should almost touch the center of your screen. See Figure D-45. Once the screen is set at the proper height, tilt it backwards just a bit. You should feel like you are looking down slightly at the screen. Your screen should be directly in front of you and parallel to your shoulders. A monitor that is tilted to one side or another makes your eyes focus at different distances, which is tiring.

FIGURE D-45: Positioning a monitor

© Cengage Learning

If you use two monitors, place your second monitor as close to the first monitor as possible, but angled so that when you turn your head slightly, you face it straight on. You might also consider moving it to the other side of your primary monitor periodically. When positioning your monitor, try to minimize the amount of glare from lights or windows that is reflected on the screen. Angle the screen away from windows. It is best not to end up facing a window where bright outdoor light can interfere with the way your pupils need to dilate for the brightness of your computer screen. If glare is a problem in your work area, you can purchase an antiglare screen that fits

over your monitor. Keeping the surface of your monitor free of dust can also cut down on glare. Notebook computers present an ergonomic problem because the screen and keyboard are typically attached to each other. Placement becomes a compromise between the best viewing angle and the best typing height. When possible, use an external keyboard and mouse with your notebook computer to achieve a more ergonomic work area.

People who wear bifocal and trifocal lenses tend to focus on the computer screen through the bottom of the lens. In order to do this, wearers raise their chins to view the screen. This puts stress on neck muscles and causes headaches. To avoid this situation, bifocal and trifocal wearers might have to lower their screens or ask their optometrist for eyewear dedicated to viewing the computer screen.

One of the most effective steps you can take to avoid eyestrain is to adjust the resolution of your monitor so that you can easily read the text displayed on your screen. Remember that you can make two types of adjustments. You can adjust the resolution of your monitor through the operating system. This adjustment affects window, icon, and text size globally. Refer to Figure D-46. LCD screens have a native resolution that displays one pixel for each tiny light in the display matrix. Selecting a resolution lower than a screen's native resolution forces the display device to interpolate pixels. This results in a slightly fuzzy display.

FIGURE D-46: Changing screen resolution

Used with permission from Microsoft

If you use more than one monitor, they will be shown here; select one.

The monitor's native resolution is usually the highest setting.

Once your monitor is set to its native resolution, you might find that the text on Web pages and in documents is too small to view comfortably. In that situation, you can adjust the zoom level within various applications. For example, you might set your browser to display larger text, and set your word processor to display text at 125 percent or 150 percent. Figure D-47 shows how a document in a word processor compares at two different zoom levels.

FIGURE D-47: Change zoom level to increase size of text on the screen

Zoom is set at 100%

Used with permission from Microsoft

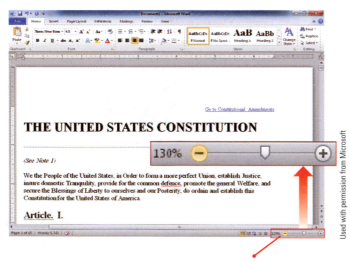

To enlarge the text, Zoom to 130% but less text will be visible on the screen

Used with permission from Microsoft

Back Pain

Back pain can be caused by many factors, including poor posture and careless lifting of heavy objects. Doctors and physical therapists more commonly use the term *flex-forward position* to describe the sitting posture shared by many computer users. The layman's term *computer slump* refers to the posture of sitting hunched over a computer keyboard with your neck craned forward. See Figure D-48. Habitual slouching can lead to stiffness and muscle tenderness. Left uncorrected, the problem can cause nerve irritation that spreads down the arms and back. Back problems caused by habitual flex-forward posture are sometimes referred to as T4 syndrome, after the fourth cervical vertebra that is most affected.

FIGURE D-48: Incorrect posture

© Cengage Learning

The key to comfort while working on a computer is keeping your shoulders relaxed so that tense muscles don't generate headaches and stiffness. If the arm rests on your chair make your shoulders rise, you should remove the armrests or get another chair. Conventional wisdom about sitting straight has been challenged recently by a body of evidence that indicates the best position for computer work is with your upper torso leaning back slightly. With your torso at a 100-110 degree angle, the back of your chair helps to support your spine.

> **The key to comfort while working on a computer is keeping your shoulders relaxed so that tense muscles don't generate headaches and stiffness.**

Carrying a heavy notebook computer can also contribute to back problems. To lighten your load, try to reduce the number of peripheral devices you carry. Consider toting your notebook computer in a backpack instead of a shoulder bag. Be sure the backpack provides the proper protection for your notebook computer. When traveling, place your notebook computer in a wheeled carrier.

Sedentary Lifestyle

People who live and work in digital cultures tend to spend many hours each day in sedentary pursuits, such as watching television and using computers. Many researchers believe that there is a link between our increasingly sedentary lifestyle and a steady climb in obesity and cardiovascular disease. To counteract the effects of a sedentary lifestyle, it is important to exercise and eat right. A good balance of stretching and cardiovascular exercise can help you keep physically fit and has the additional benefit of helping to prevent repetitive stress injuries and back pain. See Figure D-49.

FIGURE D-49: Get exercise

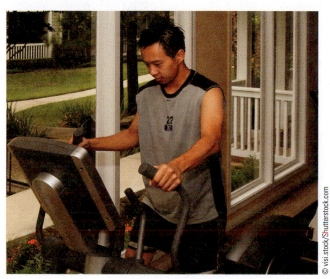

© visi.stock/Shutterstock.com

Sitting still for long periods of time, especially in positions that limit blood circulation, can be a health risk, similar to the risk of long-haul air travel. A condition called deep vein thrombosis is the formation of blood clots that commonly affect veins in the legs. Symptoms include pain, swelling, and redness in the affected area. Deep vein thrombosis requires treatment to prevent life-threatening complications if the clot moves to the heart. Although the condition is not common in young people, good work habits can help you maintain healthy circulation. For example, your chair should allow for good circulation to your legs. Make sure there are at least two inches of clearance between your calf and the front of your chair. Your thighs should be parallel to the ground to allow for good blood flow; if necessary, use a footrest to raise your feet and reduce the pressure on the backs of your thighs.

> **Many researchers believe that there is a link between our increasingly sedentary lifestyle and a steady climb in obesity and cardiovascular disease.**

To combat potential health hazards associated with computer use, you should try to take breaks periodically, say, every 20 minutes or at least once every hour. At minimum, try the 20/20/20 break: Every 20 minutes, take 20 seconds and look 20 feet away. Longer breaks of two to five minutes are more effective. During a longer break, stand up to change your circulation. Rest your eyes by focusing on distant objects. Gently rotate and stretch your wrists, shoulders, and neck. Break reminder software, such as RSIGuard and open source Workrave, can help you remember when it is time to take a break from your work. See Figure D-50.

FIGURE D-50: An example of break software

Courtesy of Workrave

> **... try the 20/20/20 break: Every 20 minutes, take 20 seconds and look 20 feet away.**

In conclusion, computer use can be hazardous to your health if you do not follow the guidelines set forth by health experts and described in this Talking Points section. But if you take proper care, you can work to improve your health and avoid computer-related health problems.

Expand the Ideas

1. Have you found that using computers has impacted your health in any way? Describe what you have experienced and any steps you have taken to improve the situation and follow good practices for healthy computing.

2. What steps have you taken to set up your computer so that it is ergonomically positioned? Explain how your actions have helped your situation and improved your health.

3. Do you make a habit of spending long hours in front of the computer? Do you try to take frequent breaks? How difficult is it to adjust your working habits to be healthier as you work at the computer? Do you believe that healthy habits will prevent computer-related injuries? Research current products and techniques for helping people work healthier at their computers.

Key Terms & Unit Review

Key Terms

Backup
Benchmark
Binary digit
Binary number system
Bit
Bus
Byte
Cache
Cache memory
Capacitor
Central processing unit (CPU)
Character data
Chip
Clock speed
Compiler
Computer chip
Computer programmer
Cycle
Data representation
Digital data
Digitize
DIMM (dual inline memory module)
DIP (dual inline package)
Directory
EEPROM
Exa-
Exabyte (EB)
File date
File extension
File format
File management
File management program
File path
File size
File specification
File tag
Filename
Filenaming conventions
Filename extension
Folder
Front side bus (FSB)
Giga-
Gigabit (Gb)
Gigabyte (GB)
Integrated circuit (IC)
Interpreter
Kilo-
Kilobit (Kb)
Kilobyte (KB)
Library
Mega-
Megabit (Mb)
Megabyte (MB)
Microprocessor
Motherboard
multi-core processor
Nanosecond
Native file format
Nested folder
Numeric data
Object code
Path
Peta-
Petabyte (PB)
PGA (pin-grid array)
Pixel
Processor
Processor cycle
RAM (Random Access Memory)
RAM cache
ROM (Read Only Memory)
ROM BIOS (basic input/ output system)
Root directory
SDRAM (synchronous DRAM)
Source code
Subdirectory
Subfolder
Swap file
Tera-
Terabyte (TB)
Virtual memory
Windows Explorer
Word size
Zetta-
Zettabyte (ZB)

Unit Review

1. Review the bold terms in this unit. Then pick 10 terms that are the least familiar to you. Be sure that you can use your own words to define the terms you have selected.

2. Describe how the binary number system uses only 1s and 0s to represent numbers.

3. Describe three types of information that are stored with a file and the importance of a file extension.

4. Describe the difference between the Save and the Save As commands.

5. Describe three file management tasks that might best be accomplished using a file management program, such as Windows Explorer.

6. Using a sample file path from your own computer, describe a file path and how it describes the location of a file on the storage medium.

7. List five tips to follow when organizing files on your hard drive.

8. Explain the difference between bits and bytes, and the technical meaning of common prefixes, such as kilo, mega, giga, peta, and tera. What aspect of a computer system does each measure?

9. Make sure that you understand the meaning of the following measurement terms: KB, Kb, MB, Mb, GB, Gb, PB, TB, ZB, MHz, GHz, and ns.

10. List three different types of memory and briefly describe how each one works as you use your computer.

Concepts Review

Select the best answer.

1. The _____ is a unique set of characters that identifies a file and should describe its contents.
   a. folder
   b. file size
   c. file path
   d. filename

2. The main directory of a disk is sometimes referred to as the _____ directory.
   a. first
   b. root
   c. tree
   d. virtual

3. A file's location is defined by a file _____, which includes the drive letter, folder(s), filename, and extension.
   a. path
   b. extension
   c. name
   d. letter

4. A _____ further describes the file contents, and often lets you know which application can be used to open the file.
   a. file extension
   b. folder
   c. drive letter
   d. drive map

5. The main hard drive is usually referred to as drive _____ or as Local Disk.
   a. A
   b. B
   c. C
   d. D

6. Use the _____ command to specify a name and storage device for a file and then store it on a storage medium.
   a. Save As
   b. New folder
   c. Open
   d. Select

7. Which of the following is not a valid default folder supplied with Windows?
   a. Documents
   b. Pictures
   c. Budgets
   d. Music

8. Which of the following companies is a major manufacturer of computer chips?
   a. Yahoo
   b. Apple
   c. Intel
   d. Google

9. The _____ number system represents numeric data as a series of 0s and 1s.
   a. integrated
   b. decimal
   c. binary
   d. singular

10. _____ data is text, numbers, graphics, sound, and video that has been converted into discrete digits, such as 0s and 1s.
    a. Digital
    b. Number
    c. Multimedia
    d. Internet

11. Which of the following is not a valid term?
    a. Bigabyte
    b. Petabyte
    c. Exabyte
    d. Terabyte

12. A series of eight bits is referred to as a(n) _____.
    a. word
    b. byte
    c. megabyte
    d. kilobit

13. The terms computer chip, microchip, and chip are all synonymous with the term _____ circuit.
    a. digital
    b. chip
    c. integrated
    d. silicon

14. The _____ size refers to the number of bits that a processor can manipulate at one time.
    a. CPU
    b. bit
    c. cycle
    d. word

15. The chip _____ is what protects the chip and connects the chip to the motherboard.
    a. word size
    b. packaging
    c. power
    d. circuitry

16. A single processor that contains circuitry for more than one processing unit is called a(n) _____ processor.
    a. AMD
    b. semiconducting
    c. Intel
    d. multi-core

17. _____ is a temporary holding area for data, application program instructions, and the operating system.
    a. EEPROM
    b. ROM
    c. Virtual memory
    d. RAM

18. The decimal number 4 is represented as _____ in the binary number system.
    a. 40
    b. 1876
    c. 1
    d. 100

19. A computer specification with 2 GB Dual Channel DDR2 SDRAM at 1600 MHz (max 4 GB) currently has _____ of random access memory installed.
    a. 2 gigabytes
    b. 1600 megahertz
    c. 4 gigabytes
    d. 2DDR

20. If a program exceeds the allocated space in RAM, the operating system uses an area of the hard drive called _____ to store parts of a program or data file until they are needed.
    a. EEPROM
    b. virtual memory
    c. ROM
    d. RAM

Independent Challenges

Independent Challenge 1

How will you organize the information that you store on your hard drive? Your hard drive or other storage medium is your electronic filing cabinet for all your work and papers. You can create many different filing systems. The way you set up your folders guides your work and helps you keep your ideas and projects organized so that you can work efficiently with your computer. Take some time to think about the work that you do, the types of documents or files you will be creating, and then decide how you will organize your files and folders.

Windows provides a feature that allows you to customize the icons for your folder shortcuts. You can use these custom icons to help you organize your folders even more. Windows supplies a large collection of icons that you can apply to each folder. Start Windows Explorer and be sure you are viewing the folders listed under a user name and not the folders shown in the libraries. You must click the user name, and then drill down from there. Once you get to the folder, right-click it in the left pane of Windows Explorer, and then click Properties (click Customize if you are using Windows Vista). In the Properties dialog box, click Change Icon. See Figure D-51. Note: in Windows 7 you cannot change the folder icon if you access the folder through a library.

FIGURE D-51: Changing folder icons

Used with permission from Microsoft

If you are using a Mac, you can also customize the icons. Every volume (disk), application, file, and folder on your Mac appears as an icon. For example, your internal hard drive looks like a hard drive, removable drives look like removable drives, and optical discs such as CDs and DVDs look like discs. File icons generally show a document with an application logo that lets you know what application was used to create it or what can be used to open it, such as a graphic editor or Word. To make changes to the icons, you work through the File menu and use the Get Info command.

For this Independent Challenge:

1. Read each of the following plans for organizing files and folders on a hard drive or other storage medium and comment on the advantages and disadvantages of each plan.
   a. Create a folder for each file you create.
   b. Store all the files in the root directory.
   c. Store all files in the Documents folder.
   d. Create a folder for each application you plan to use and store only documents you generate with that application in each folder.
   e. Create folders for broad types of documents such as memos, flyers, letters, budgets, art, photographs, and data, then store all related files within the folders.
   f. Create folders based on specific topics such as business, personal, household, and school, then store all related documents and files within the respective folders.
   g. Create a new folder for each month and store all files or documents created in that month in the appropriate folder.

2. Write a summary of how you plan to organize the folders and files on your hard drive or other storage medium, and explain why you chose the method you did.

3. Refer back to Figure D-51 and describe how you might use icons to help you identify the types of files in the folders.

Independent Challenge 2

You can use Windows Explorer or any file management program on your computer to explore and find specific files and folders on your hard drive.

For this Independent Challenge:

1a. Start Windows Explorer, then click the Computer icon. List the devices under Computer. Identify each device as a Network Device, Hard Drive, or Removable Storage. Windows Explorer lets you organize and view applications, files, folders, discs, and memory cards located on the hard drive of your PC, and on shared drives on your network.

1b. If you are using a Mac, use the Finder program. The Finder is the blue smiling face icon on the Dock. Finder lets you organize and view applications, files, folders, discs, and memory cards located on the hard drive of your Mac, and on shared drives on your network.

2. Pick any five files on the computer that you typically use and write the full path for each one. Refer to Figure D-52. Identify the programs that were used to create each of the files you found.

© Cengage Learning

3. Open the Documents folder on the Local Disk C: (if not available, find the folder that has your documents). List how many folders are in the Documents folder (or alternate folder if you selected one) on your hard drive.

4. Open one of the folders in the Documents folder (or alternate folder), click Views, then display the Details view. Are file extensions showing? If so, list them and identify which programs would open those files. Look at the folder using at least two views. Explain the differences between the views.

5. How many different types of files can you find on your hard drive? List up to 10.

Independent Challenge 3

How powerful is your computer? Some computers are more powerful than others because they can store more data and process data faster. To find out how your home, work, or lab computer stacks up, you'll need to know a few of its specifications.

For this Independent Challenge:

Check your computer's specifications by doing the following:

1. Start your computer.

2a. If you are using a Windows computer: Click the Start button, then click Control Panel. Click the System icon or click the System link to open the System Properties dialog box. Depending on your version of Windows, you may have slightly different commands to open the System Properties dialog box or System and Security window. You might have to click System and Maintenance or System and Security to view this page. If you see a dialog box with tabs, make sure the General tab is displayed. If you see a page, be sure you are looking at the System page. You will see basic information about your computer system, including the operating system, the manufacturer and model, the processor, and the installed RAM.

2b. If your computer is a Mac running MAC OS X: click the Apple icon on the menu bar located at the top of the desktop, then select About This Mac. In the About This Mac window that opens, you will see the Mac OS version as well as the processor speed (in GHz) and the processor series (G4, G5) for your Macintosh. Additionally, it will list

the amount of memory (RAM) installed. Click More Info, and on the right side of the window that opens, click the arrow next to Hardware to view the list of devices.

3. Record information about your computer similar to the information listed in Table D-5.

TABLE D-5: Computer specifications

	Your computer	Notes
Computer model and manufacturer:		
Processor manufacturer and model:		
Processor speed:		
Number of cores in the processor:		
Installed RAM:		
RAM capacity:		
System type:		
Windows Experience Index: (for Windows PCs)		
Operating system version:		

© Cengage Learning

4a. Just to get an idea of other hardware you have attached to your Windows computer, click the link or icon for Device Manager. (You might have to click the Hardware tab first.)

4b. If you are using a Mac, open Finder. Expand the icons to see the display adapters, the disk drives, keyboard, pointing devices, ports, and processors. List five of the devices. Tell why each device is connected to the computer. For example, you might see a 3Com wireless network card and state it is used to connect the computer to the Internet, or you might see a Pioneer DVD-RW DVR-107D ATA device and state it is used to read files from and write files to a DVD.

_____

_____

_____

_____

5. When you're done, close all open dialog boxes.

Guide to Buying a Computer

As you prepare to buy a computer, there are a lot of decisions you have to make. This book is designed to help you build the knowledge base you need to purchase a computer. In this unit, you were introduced to file management and digital electronics. You learned that you can enhance the performance of your computer depending on the processor and memory that you include in your computer. The specifications can be referred to as the architecture of your computer.

Each unit in this book covers topics that can help you understand the type of computer you need, the add-on parts you might want to buy, and the software and services that will enhance your computing experience, such as Internet access, software purchases, and so forth. After each unit, you will be asked to answer questions by completing a worksheet. By the end of the book, your Guide to Buying a Computer worksheet will provide comprehensive information about buying a computer.

To help you organize the information you will need when you are ready to buy a computer, you should complete the following activities:

1. Review the specifications for the fictitious computer ad in Figure D-53.

   Referring to the computer in the advertisement, what type of processor and how much memory are included with this computer? Is this a powerful computer?

2. Refer again to the advertisement in Figure D-53. Based on what you learned about processors, who might use a computer with this power?

3. If you have an older computer, you might ask what makes more economic sense—to upgrade your older computer to make it more powerful or to buy a new computer. Some parts are easy to add or change, whereas others are not. Table D-6 summarizes the most popular computer equipment upgrades, and indicates their average time to install and the difficulty level of the installation.

4. Two columns have been left blank for you to complete. Log onto the Internet or go to the library and review recent computer magazines to complete the "Cost" column and the "Whether you would consider replacing this part" column?

FIGURE D-53: Fake computer ad

- Intel Core 2 Quad Q9650 processor 3.0 GHz, 1333 MHz FSB
- 12 MB L2 cache
- 4 GB DDR2-800 MHz dual channel SDRAM (max 8GB)
- 500 GB SATA HD (7200 rpm)
- 16X max. DVD+/-R/RW SuperMulti drive
- 20" WUXGA monitor
- 512 MB NVIDIA GeForce graphics card
- Creative Sound Blaster X-Fi Xtreme Audio sound card
- Logitech speakers
- Mouse and keyboard
- Storage bay: Portable Media Drive Bay
- 6 USB ports: 2 front, 4 back
- 2 IEEE 1394
- 1 network port (RJ45 connector)
- 7 expansion slots
- Windows 7 operating system
- Home/small business software bundle
- 1-year limited warranty

© Cengage Learning; © 300dpi/Shutterstock.com; Used with permission from Microsoft

TABLE D-6: Popular computer equipment upgrades

Upgrade	Time	Cost (US$)	Difficulty	Would you consider replacing this part? (Yes/No) Why? Why not?
Replace processor	1–5 hours		Difficult and not Recommended	
Add memory	30–60 minutes		Moderate	
Add external hard drive	5–10 minutes		Easy	
Replace internal hard drive	1–2 hours		Somewhat difficult	
Replace graphics card	1 hour		Moderate	
Switch to wireless keyboard and mouse	5 minutes		Easy	
Add USB hub or digital camera memory card reader	5 minutes		Easy	
Add second display screen	30 minutes		Easy	
Add or replace speakers	5–10 minutes		Easy	
Replace internal CD, BD, or DVD drive	1 hour		Moderate	

© Cengage Learning

5. As you continue to work through this book, you will learn more about personal computer systems. You will have the opportunity to answer more questions and complete other worksheets with information that will help you when it is time to buy a computer. To help you think about the processor and RAM you need for a personal computer system, complete this portion of the Guide to Buying a Computer worksheet.

Guide to Buying a Computer: Processor and RAM considerations

Questions to consider	Pages where the topic is covered in this book (refer back to these pages to read more about the topic)	Notes (add additional comments, clarifications, or ideas about each topic)
PROCESSOR CONSIDERATIONS		
Processor manufacturer?		
Processor model		
Processor speed		
Details about the processor		
Word size?		
32 bit?		
64 bit?		
Bus speed?		
Clock speed?		
How many cores?		
Single-core processor		
Dual-core processor		
Multi-core processor		
RAM CONSIDERATIONS		
How much RAM?		
RAM cache type and size:		
Level 1 cache (L1)?		
Level 2 cache (L2)?		
RAM speed?		

6. Write any questions you have about buying a processor or RAM on the lines that follow. As you continue to work through this book, check back to see if these questions have been answered.

My Questions

_____

_____

_____

_____

Visual Workshop

Understanding the specifications listed for processors often seems overwhelming. When you buy a computer, you can now find processors by manufacturer (Intel or AMD), by brand (Atom and Xeon, or Phenom and Opteron), and by model names. You can choose from processor families, such as 2nd Gen Intel Core i7. More often than not, you will buy a computer, rather than buy only a processor. It is important to know about processors, however, so you can make an informed decision about the processor in each computer you are considering buying. Figure D-54 shows a Web page from the Intel.com Web site advertising high-end processors and a Web page from the AMD.com Web site advertising some Phenom processors. If you go to these Web sites, you can see that these two processor manufacturers have a very large selection of processors for many different applications.

FIGURE D-54: Web sites of popular processor manufacturers

1. Log on to the Internet or use any resource available to find these or similar Web pages describing current processors available for desktop and laptop computers. Find two featured processors at each site and list four key specifications for each. Write a brief statement, using the terms you learned in this unit, to explain each feature.

2. Find two computer ads on the Internet or in a local paper. Identify the processors for those computers. Can you find the processors on the Intel or AMD Web site? Explain your findings.

3. Both Intel and AMD also sell personal computer systems from their Web sites. Each has a "Help me find the right PC" feature (although the exact name may be different. Use this tool to find two computers from each manufacturer. Write a brief description of your search results and include the specifications for each computer.

Getting Started with CourseMate

Learning Objectives

1. Explain why you would use a CourseMate
2. Know how to access the CourseMate for this book
3. Know how to use CourseMate study tools

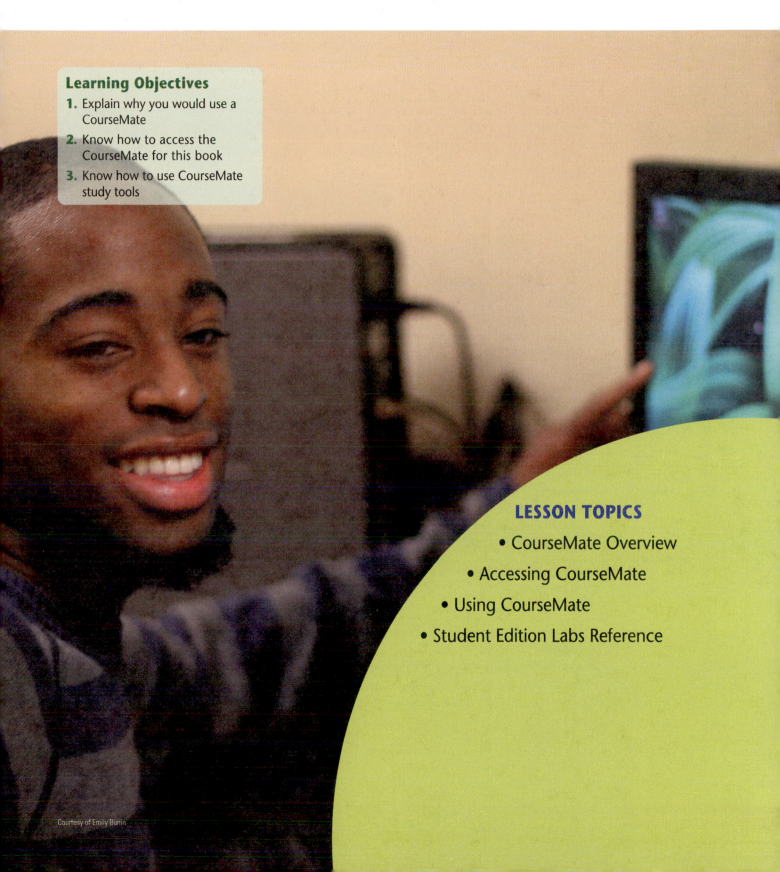

LESSON TOPICS

• CourseMate Overview

• Accessing CourseMate

• Using CourseMate

• Student Edition Labs Reference

Courtesy of Emily Bunin

CourseMate Overview

Cengage Learning's CourseMate brings course concepts to life with interactive learning, study, and exam preparation tools that support the printed textbook. CourseMate includes an integrated eBook, and interactive teaching and learning tools. These include quizzes, flashcards, videos, and Student Edition Labs, which are an engaging collection of hands-on training activities and animations. In order to use CourseMate, you must have purchased a CourseMate access code for this book. You also need a Web browser and must be connected to the Internet. This lesson reviews the key elements of the CourseMate for this book.

DETAILS

The CourseMate for this book includes the following elements for each unit:

- **Interactive eBook**
  The eBook lets you read each unit of the book on your computer screen. You can search for specific topics or keywords, highlight text, and take notes.

- **Videos**
  The CourseMate includes short "highlight" videos for each two-page lesson in the book. Each video runs about 2 to 3 minutes long and presents highlights of the key points covered in the lesson, to help draw you into the topic. See Figure CM-1.

- **Glossary and Flashcards**
  Use the Glossary and Flashcard features to help you master the key terms in each unit. The Glossary provides a list of key terms and their definitions; the Flash Cards present key terms on one side of a digital card and definitions on the other. See Figure CM-2.

- **Concepts Review**
  The CourseMate includes an online version of the Concepts Review questions from the end-of-unit exercises; you can answer the questions online and get your results instantly.

- **Student Edition Labs**
  The Student Edition Labs are hands-on interactive activities to help you learn, understand, and retain key concepts about computers. The Student Edition Labs include animations, guided activities, and reinforcement questions. See Figure CM-3.

- **Games**
  Beat the Clock and Quiz Bowl games let you test your knowledge in a fun game format.

- **Practice Test**
  Interactive practice tests for each unit help you prepare for your exam.

- **And More!**
  CourseMate also has exercises from the book that you can access online and submit to your instructor. There is also a link to **CourseCasts**, which are podcasts on hot technology news. Hosted by Professor Ken Baldauf of Florida State University, CourseCasts are updated weekly so you will stay up to date with the latest technology developments.

FIGURE CM-1: Videos for each lesson bring key topics to life

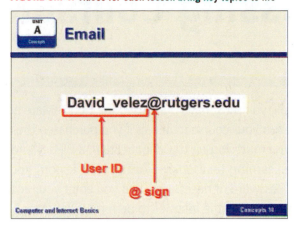

FIGURE CM-2: Use Flashcards to master key terms

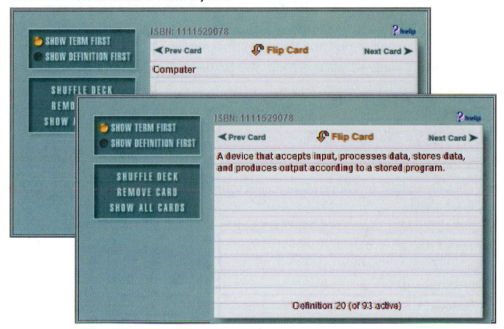

FIGURE CM-3: Student Edition Labs feature animations, guided steps, and reinforcement questions to help you learn and master key concepts

Accessing CourseMate

To access the CourseMate for this book, you must have purchased the CourseMate access code for this book. The access code might have been included in your course materials if you purchased them at your school's bookstore. Then, with your access code handy, you must log on to CengageBrain, a Web site for accessing various student resources that accompany Cengage Learning textbooks. In this lesson, you set up a CengageBrain user profile and establish a username and password, if necessary. Then you enter your access code to access the CourseMate. (Note: You must be connected to the Internet to perform these steps.)

STEPS

1. **Open your browser, type http:// login.cengagebrain.com in your browser's address bar, then press [Enter]**
   The Login page for the CengageBrain site opens. See Figure CM-4.

TROUBLE

If you don't have a CengageBrain user-name and pass-word, click Create an Account, then follow the prompts to create one.

2. **Type your CengageBrain username and password in the Log In section of the screen**
   The Find your Textbook or Materials page opens.

3. **Type your access code in the box below Have Another Product to Register?, then click Register**
   The CengageBrain site accepts your access code and the Computer Concepts Illustrated 9th Edition cover and title appear under My Courses & Materials. See Figure CM-5.

4. **Click Open next to CourseMate for Parsons/Oja Computer Concepts Illustrated 9e CourseMate**
   The CourseMate page opens. See Figure CM-6.

FIGURE CM-4: CengageBrain Log In screen

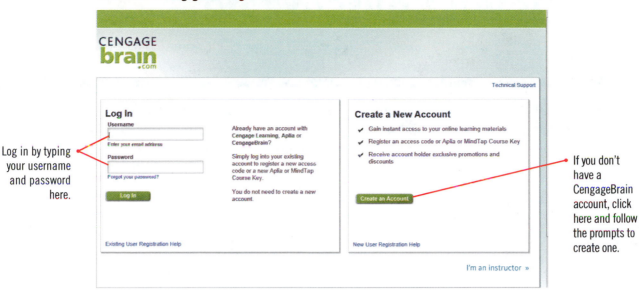

Log in by typing your username and password here.

If you don't have a CengageBrain account, click here and follow the prompts to create one.

FIGURE CM-5: My Home page, with Computer Concepts Illustrated CourseMate added

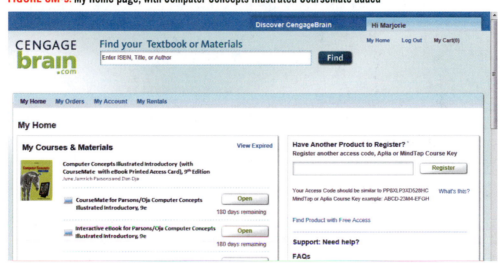

FIGURE CM-6: CourseMate Welcome page

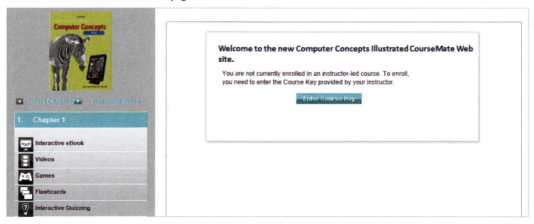

Using CourseMate

CourseMate is a great study tool that will help you learn and master the content you need to succeed in this course. In addition to interactive learning and study aids, CourseMate comes with Engagement Tracker, a tool that lets your instructor monitor student engagement in the course. Your instructor might provide you with a Course Key, which you will need to enter in order to use Engagement Tracker. (If your instructor chooses not to use Engagement Tracker, you can still access all the content on CourseMate.) In this lesson, you learn the basics of using CourseMate.

STEPS

TROUBLE
Skip to Step 3 if your instructor did not provide you with a Course Key.

1. **If your instructor provided you with a Course Key, click Enter Course Key**
   The Enter Your Course Key dialog box opens, as shown in Figure CM-7.

2. **Type your Course Key, then click Submit**

3. **Click Select Chapter, just below the book cover on the left side of the screen**
   The full table of contents for the book appears in the Select Chapter window. You can open this window anytime you want to access the content for a particular unit.

4. **Click outside the Select a Chapter window , click eBook, then click Access the eBook**
   After a moment, a new window opens and displays an eBook version of this book. You can navigate through the eBook content using the Table of Contents, glossary, or index. You can search for words or phrases, and you can annotate the text.

5. **Click the Close button on the eBook title bar**
   The eBook closes, and your screen displays the CourseMate window again.

6. **Click Videos in the Navigation pane**
   The main window displays a series of video windows. You can click any video window to start that video. Figure CM-8 shows a snapshot from a sample video.

7. **Explore the other CourseMate elements by clicking the remaining items in the navigation pane**

8. **Click the Close button in your browser's title bar**
   Your browser and CourseMate close.

FIGURE CM-7: Enter Your Course Key dialog box

Enter Your Course Key

To enroll in an instructor-led course, enter the Course Key provided by your instructor.

[   ]

Cancel   Submit

FIGURE CM-8: Videos provide animations on key concepts covered in each lesson

CourseMate

Student Edition Labs Reference

The Student Edition Labs provide hands-on interactive activities to help you learn, understand, and retain many of the concepts presented in the book. These hands-on interactive activities include animations, activities, and reinforcement questions. This page lists all the Student Edition Labs that are available in this book's CourseMate.

Student Labs Available in CourseMate

E-mail	Advanced Database Lab
Using Input Devices	Binary Numbers
Peripheral Devices	Managing Files and Folders
Maintaining a Hard Disk Drive	Networking Basics
Understanding the Motherboard	Wireless Networking
Using Windows	Connecting to the Internet
Word Processing	Keeping Your Computer Virus Free
Spreadsheets	Protecting Your Privacy Online
Databases	Backing Up Your Computer
Presentation Software	Getting the Most Out of the Internet
Working with Graphics	Creating Web Pages
Working with Video	Web Design Principles
Working with Audio	E-Commerce
Project Management	Careers and Technology: Getting Ahead
Installing and Uninstalling Software	Visual Programming
Advanced Spreadsheets	Computer Ethics

Glossary

3D graphics software Provides a set of tools for creating wireframe drawings that represent three-dimensional objects.

Access time The estimated time for a storage device to locate data on a disk, usually measured in milliseconds.

Accounting software A category of software that helps you keep a record of monetary transactions and investments.

Analog data Data that is represented using an infinite scale of values, in contrast to digital data, which is represented as discrete digits, such as 0s and 1s.

App A program such as a game, calendar, stock market tracker, traffic or weather monitor, or news feed designed to run on mobile devices such as smartphones and tablet computers. *Also called* mobile app and mobile application.

Application software Computer programs that help you perform a specific task such as word processing. *Also called* application programs, applications, or programs.

ASCII (American Standard Code for Information Interchange) A code that represents characters as a series of 1s and 0s, making it possible to transfer data between computers.

Audio editing software A category of software that includes sound playback as well as recording capabilities. Menus provide additional digital editing features, such as speed control, volume adjustments, clipping, and mixing of sounds.

Backup A copy of your files made for safekeeping.

BD (Blu-ray Disc) A high-capacity disc for storing large quantities of digital content, such as high-definition video.

BD drive A drive that plays Blu-ray discs.

Benchmark A test used to measure computer hardware or software performance.

Binary digit The smallest unit of information handled by a computer; can hold one of two values, either a 0 or a 1. Eight bits make up a byte, which can represent a letter or number. *See* Bit.

Binary number system A method for representing numbers using only two digits, 0 and 1; as compared with the decimal system, which uses ten digits: 0, 1, 2, 3, 4, 5, 6, 7, 8, and 9.

Bit The smallest unit of information handled by a computer; can hold one of two values, either a 0 or a 1. Eight bits make up a byte, which can represent a letter or number; short for binary digit.

Bit depth The number of bits that determines the range of possible colors that can be assigned to each pixel. For example, an 8-bit color depth can create 256 colors. *Also called* color depth.

Blog Derived from the phrase "WeB LOG," refers to a personal journal focusing on a single topic or covering a variety of issues posted on the Web for access by the general public.

Blu-ray disc *See* BD.

Blu-ray drive *See* BD drive.

Boot process The sequence of events that occurs within a computer system between the time the user starts the computer and the time it is ready to process commands.

Bootstrap A program stored in ROM that loads and initializes the operating system on a computer.

Browser A program that communicates with a Web server and displays Web pages.

Buffer The area of computer memory that holds data from one device while it is waiting to be transferred to another device.

Bus An electronic pathway that carries the electronic signals between the electronic parts of a computer.

Byte An 8-bit unit of information that represents a single character.

Cable A wire used to connect a peripheral device to a computer through a port.

Cable modem A communications device that can be used to connect a computer to the Internet via the cable TV infrastructure.

Cache Special high-speed memory that gives the CPU rapid access to data that would otherwise be accessed from memory elsewhere on the motherboard. *Also called* RAM cache or cache memory.

Cache memory *See* Cache.

CAD software A special type of 3D graphics software designed for architects and engineers who use computers to create blueprints and product specifications. *Also called* computer-aided design software.

Capacitor The electronic parts in a chip that hold the bits that represent data.

Card reader A device that transfers data to or from a computer.

CD (compact disc) An optical storage medium that can store up to 700 MB of data. There are a variety of CDs including CD-ROM, CD-R, and CD-RW.

CD drive A storage device that uses laser technology to read data from a CD-ROM.

CD-R disc An acronym for compact disc-recordable; a CD disc using optical disc technology that allows the user to create CD-ROMs and audio CDs.

CD-ROM disc An optical storage media that is read only and that can store up to 700 MB of data.

CD-RW disc An acronym for compact disc-rewritable; a CD disc using optical disc technology that allows the user to write data onto a CD, then change that data.

CD-writer A general term for recordable CD technologies such as CD-R and CD-RW.

Central processing unit *See* CPU.

Character data Letters, symbols, or numerals that will not be used in arithmetic operations (name, social security number, etc.).

Chat group A discussion in which a group of people communicates by typing messages to each other online simultaneously.

Chip *See* Computer chip.

Clip art Graphics designed to be inserted into documents, Web pages, and worksheets, usually available in CD-ROM or Web-based collections.

Clock speed The pace for executing instructions as set by the processor clock specified in megahertz (MHz) or gigahertz (GHz).

Cloud Mass storage for programs and data on remote computers connected to the Internet or other network.

Cloud computing A method of offering Internet-accessible computing services ranging from office productivity applications to complex corporate data processing.

Cloudware Software applications that are not installed locally on your computer but rather installed on the Web and used while online through a browser. *Also called* Web apps.

Color depth The number of bits that determines the range of possible colors that can be assigned to each pixel. For example, an 8-bit color depth can create 256 colors. *Also called* bit depth.

Commercial software Copyrighted computer applications sold to consumers for profit.

CompactFlash (CF) card A solid-state storage device that is about the size of a matchbook and provides high storage capacities and access speeds; includes a built-in controller that reads and writes data within the solid-state grid; ideal for use with high-end digital cameras.

Compiler Software that translates a program written in a high-level language into low-level instructions before the program is executed.

Compression utility Software that reduces file size for quick transmission or efficient storage.

Computer An electronic device that accepts input, processes data, stores data, and produces output.

Computer-aided design software (CAD) *See* CAD software.

Computer-aided music software Helps musicians compose, edit, and print the notes for compositions. For non-musicians, designed to generate unique music simply by selecting the musical style, instruments, key, and tempo.

Computer chip A very thin slice of semiconducting material, such as silicon and germanium. *Also called* integrated circuit.

Computer file A named collection of data (such as a computer program, document, or graphic) that exists on a storage medium, such as a hard drive, flash drive, CD, or DVD. *Also called* file or data file.

Computer language Tools that allow a programmer to write instructions or software that a computer can execute. *Also called* programming language.

Computer network A collection of computers and related devices, connected in a way that allows them to share resources including data, hardware, and software.

Computer platform A computer system's underlying hardware and software, in particular, its processor and operating system; the two dominant computer platforms today for desktop and laptop computers are PC, sometimes called the Windows platform, and Mac, which is the Macintosh OS by Apple Computer, Inc.

Computer program Detailed, step-by-step instructions that tell a computer how to solve a problem or carry out a task. *Also called* program.

Computer programmer A person who codes or writes computer programs.

Computer system The hardware, peripheral devices, and software working together to input data, process data, store data, and produce output.

Concurrent-use license A software license agreement that is priced per copy and allows a specific number of copies to be used at the same time.

Copyright A form of legal protection that grants certain exclusive rights to the author of a program or the owner of the copyright.

Copyright notice A line such as "Copyright 2014 ACME Co." that identifies a copyright holder.

CPU (central processing unit) The main processing unit in a computer, consisting of circuits that processes data. *Also called* the "brain" of a computer.

Cursor A symbol that marks the user's place on the screen and shows where typing will appear. *Also called* insertion point.

Cycle The smallest unit of time a processor can recognize. For example, 2.8 GHz means that the processor's clock operates at a speed of 2.8 billion cycles per second.

Data In the context of computing and data management, the symbols that a computer uses to represent facts and ideas.

Data bus An electronic pathway or circuit that connects the electronic components (such as the processor and RAM) on a computer's motherboard.

Data file A named collection of data (such as a computer program, document, or graphic) that exists on a storage medium, such as a hard drive, flash drive, CD, or DVD. *Also called* computer file or file.

Data representation The use of electrical signals, marks, or binary digits to represent character, numeric, visual, or audio data.

Data transfer rate The amount of data that a storage device can move from a storage medium to computer memory in one second.

Database A collection of data that is stored electronically as a series of records in tables.

Database software A category of software designed for tasks associated with maintaining and accessing data stored in data files.

Demoware Commercial software available as a trial version and distributed for free. Often comes preinstalled on new computers, but it is limited in some way until paid for.

Desktop computer A category of computer small enough to fit on a desk but is too big to carry around and has attached, rather than built-in, keyboard, display, and pointing device.

Desktop gadget A utility program on a computer's desktop used to display information such as a clock, calendar, calculator, news aggregators, notes, and weather. *Also called* a gadget.

Desktop publishing software (DPT) A category of software used to create high-quality output suitable for commercial printing. DPT software provides precise control over layout.

Desktop widget *See* Widget.

Device driver The software that provides the computer with the means to control a peripheral device.

Digital Any system that works with discrete data, such as 0s and 1s, in contrast to analog.

Digital camera A peripheral input device that records photographic images in digital format.

Digital content Any text, graphics, video, audio, or any data and information stored in a file and available for transmission, viewing or playing, and storage via a computer.

Digital convergence The trend to blend several technologies that have distinct functionalities into a single product, such as smartphones that combine voice communication, text messaging, email, Web browsing, cameras, and GPS.

Digital data Text, numbers, graphics, sound, and video that have been converted into discrete digits, such as 0s and 1s.

Digital device A device that works with discrete (distinct or separate) numbers or digits.

Digital electronics Circuitry that is designed to work with digital signals.

Digital media player A peripheral device that can be attached to a personal computer system to transfer and play music and photo files.

Digital revolution An ongoing process of social, political, and economic change brought about by digital technology, such as computers and the Internet.

Digital technology Technologies that work using digital electronics such as computers, communications networks, the Web, and digitization.

Digital versatile disc *See* DVD.

Digitization *See* Digitize.

Digitize To convert text, numbers, sound, photos, and video to a digital format that can be processed by a computer, through the use of a scanner, camera, or other input device.

DIMM (dual in-line memory module) A long, slim memory chip package that has gold pins that provide the electronic connection between the chip and other computer parts.

DIP (dual in-line package) A chip configuration characterized by a rectangular body with numerous plugs along its edge.

Direct access The ability of a storage device (such as a hard drive) to go directly to a specific storage location without having to search sequentially from a beginning location. *Also called* random access.

Directory A list of files contained on a computer storage device.

Display device The main output device for a computer; presents visual information on a screen such as a computer monitor.

Distribution media One or more discs, CDs, or other storage media that contain programs and data, which can be installed on a hard drive.

Document reader utility Computer program, such as Adobe Reader, that transforms files into a portable format that can be created and read by any computer on which it is installed.

DOS (disk operating system) The operating system software shipped with the first IBM PCs and used on millions of computers until the introduction of Microsoft Windows.

Dot pitch The diagonal distance between colored dots on a display screen. Measured in millimeters, dot pitch helps to determine the quality of an image displayed on a monitor. A smaller dot pitch means a crisper image.

Dots per inch (dpi) A measure of screen resolution and printer quality. A higher number of dots per inch indicates a higher resolution and better-quality output.

Downloading The process of transferring a copy of a file from a remote computer to a local computer's hard drive.

Dpi (dots per inch) *See* Dots per inch (dpi).

Drawing software Provides tools to draw lines, shapes, and colors that can be assembled into diagrams, corporate logos, and schematics that tend to have a flat cartoon-like quality, but are very easy to modify.

Drive bay Storage device "parking spaces" on the system unit case for a desktop computer; until these are used, they are typically hidden from view with a faceplate. *Also called* expansion bay.

Dual-core processor A single chip containing the circuitry for two processors; faster than a processor with a single core.

Duplex printer A printer that has the capability of printing on both sides of a page in a single pass.

Duty cycle Determines how many pages a printer is able to print out; is usually measured in pages per month.

DVD (digital video disc or digital versatile disc) An optical storage medium similar in appearance and technology to a CD but with higher storage capacity.

DVD authoring software Provides tools for transferring video footage from a digital video camera to a computer, deleting unwanted footage, assembling video segments in any sequence, adding special visual effects, adding a sound track, and creating a DVD.

DVD drive An optical storage device that reads data from CD-ROM and DVD discs.

DVD+R (digital versatile disc recordable) disc A type of DVD disc that stores data using recordable optical disc technology.

DVD-R (digital versatile disc recordable) disc A type of DVD disc that stores data using recordable optical disc technology.

DVD-ROM (digital versatile disc read-only memory) disc A type of DVD disc that stores data that has been permanently stamped on the disc surface.

DVD+RW (digital versatile disc rewritable) disc A type of DVD disc that stores data using rewritable optical disc technology.

DVD-RW (digital versatile disc rewritable) disc A type of DVD disc that stores data using rewritable optical disc technology.

DVD writer A device that can be used to create and copy CDs and DVDs.

EBCDIC (Extended Binary-Coded Decimal Interchange Code) A method by which digital computers, usually mainframes, use 0s and 1s to represent character data.

Educational software A category of software that helps you learn and practice new skills.

Edutainment software A category of software that is both educational and entertaining.

EEPROM (electrically erasable programmable read-only memory) A nonvolatile chip that requires no power to hold data and holds computer configuration settings, such as the date and time, hard drive capacity, number of CD/DVD drives, and RAM capacity.

Electronic mail *See* Email.

Email (electronic mail) A single electronic message, or the entire system of computers and software that handles electronic messages transmitted between computers over a communications network.

Email account A service that provides an email address and mailbox.

Email address The unique address for each mailbox on the Internet, which typically consists of a user ID, an @ symbol, and the name of the computer that maintains the mailbox.

Email attachment A separate file that is transmitted along with an email message.

Email message A message, letter, or memo that is transmitted electronically via a network.

Email software Computer program that is used to compose, send, and read email messages. Usually includes an address book to help you maintain contact information.

EULA (end-user license agreement) License agreement that is displayed on the screen when you first install software; you accept the terms of the license by clicking a designated button.

Exa- A prefix for quintillion.

Exabyte Used to identify vast amounts of data; approximately equal to 1 billion gigabytes.

Executable file A file, usually with an .exe extension, containing instructions that tell a computer how to perform a specific task.

Expansion bay Storage device "parking spaces" on the system unit case for a desktop computer; until used these are typically hidden from view with a faceplate. *Also called* drive bays.

Expansion bus The segment of the data bus that transports data between RAM and peripheral devices.

Expansion card A circuit board that is plugged into a slot on a motherboard to add extra functions, devices, or ports.

Expansion port A socket into which the user plugs a cable from a peripheral device, allowing data to pass between the computer and the peripheral device.

Expansion slot A socket or slot on a motherboard designed to hold a circuit board called an expansion card.

Favorites A list of URLs for Web sites that you can create for your browser to store so that you can revisit those sites easily.

Field The smallest meaningful unit of information contained in a data file.

File A named collection of data (such as a computer program, document, or graphic) that exists on a storage medium, such as a hard drive, flash drive, CD, or DVD. *Also called* computer file and data file.

File date Saved as part of the file information, the date on which a file was created or last modified; useful if you have created several versions of a file and want to make sure that you know which version is the most recent.

File extension A set of letters and/or numbers added to the end of a filename following a period that helps to identify the file contents or file type.

File format The method of organization used to encode and store data in a computer. Text formats include DOCX and TXT. Graphics formats include BMP, TIFF, and GIF.

File management The process of organizing files and folders on storage media.

File management program Software, such as Windows Explorer or Mac OS Finder, that helps users find files and folders on their hard drives or other storage media, as well as, rename, move, copy, and delete files.

File path *See* File specification.

File size The physical size of a file on a storage medium, usually measured in kilobytes (KB) or megabytes (MB).

File specification A combination of the drive letter, subdirectory, filename, and extension that identifies a file (for example, C:\Documents\filename.docx). *Also called* path or file path.

File tag Information that helps describe contents of a file; for example the location, camera settings, and people pictured in a photograph. Tags can be added manually by a person or automatically by software and appear when viewing file lists in Windows Explorer, as well in the file's Properties dialog box.

Filename A set of letters or numbers that identifies a file. Consists of a name followed by a period, followed by a file extension. *See* File extension.

Filename extension *See* File extension.

Filenaming conventions A set of rules established by the operating system that must be followed to create a valid filename.

Finance software Category of software to help you keep a record of monetary transactions and investments.

Folder The subdirectory, or subdivision, of a directory that can contain files or other folders.

Font A typeface or style of lettering, such as Arial, Times New Roman, and Gothic.

Format Refers to how all text, pictures, titles, and page numbers appear on the page.

Freeware Copyrighted software that is given away by the author or owner.

Front Side Bus (FSB) Refers to the circuitry that transports data to and from the processor.

Gadget A utility program on a computer's desktop used to display information such as a clock, calendar, calculator, news aggregators, notes, and weather. *Also called* desktop gadget.

General Public License (GPL) Software created under this licensing policy allows people to make copies of software for their own use, to give it to others, or to sell it.

Giga– Prefix for a billion.

Gigabit (Gb) Approximately one billion bits.

Gigabyte (GB) Approximately one billion bytes; typically used to refer to RAM and hard drive capacity.

Gigahertz (GHz) A measure of frequency equivalent to one billion cycles per second; usually used to measure speed.

Graphical user interface (GUI) A type of user interface that features on-screen objects, such as menus and icons, manipulated by a mouse. The GUI acronym is pronounced "gooey."

Graphics Any pictures, photographs, or images that can be manipulated or viewed on a computer.

Graphics card A circuit board inserted into a computer to handle the display of text, graphics, animation, and videos. *Also called* a video card.

Graphics software Computer programs for creating, editing, and manipulating images.

Graphics tablet A device that accepts input from a pressure-sensitive stylus and converts strokes into images on the screen.

Hacker A person who creates malicious computer programs sometimes to steal or damage your data or hardware or to assume your identity for financial gain.

Handheld computer A small, pocket-sized computer such as the Apple iPhone, the BlackBerry SmartPhone, and the Hewlett-Packard

iPAQ, designed to run on its own power supply and provide users with basic applications.

Hard disk drive *See* Hard drive.

Hard drive A computer storage device that contains a large-capacity hard disk sealed inside the drive case.

Hardware The electronic and mechanical devices in a computer system.

Head crash A collision between the read-write head and the surface of the hard drive platter, resulting in damage to some of the data on the disk.

Home page On a Web site, the page that is the first page you see when you go to the site. On an individual computer, the Web page that a browser displays each time it is started.

HTML (Hypertext Markup Language) A standardized programming language used to specify the format for Web page documents.

HTTP (Hypertext Transfer Protocol) A communications standard that is used to transport Web pages over the Internet.

Hyperlink Provides the fundamental tool for navigating Web pages. Click a hyperlink to jump to a location in the same Web page, open a different Web page, or go to a different Web site. *Also called* a link.

Hypertext A way of linking information through the use of text and multimedia.

Hypertext Transfer Protocol (HTTP) *See* HTTP.

Image editing software Software that provides a set of electronic pens, brushes, and paints for drawing, creating, or editing graphics such as drawings and photographs. *Also called* paint software.

Information The words, numbers, and graphics used as the basis for human actions and decisions.

Ink jet printer A nonimpact printer that creates characters or graphics by spraying liquid ink onto paper or other media.

Input As a noun, "input" means the information that is conveyed to a computer. As a verb, "input" means to enter data into a computer.

Input device A device, such as a keyboard or mouse, that gathers input and transforms it into a series of electronic signals for the computer.

Insertion point Appears on the screen as a flashing vertical bar or flashing underline and indicates where the characters you type will appear on the screen. *Also called* cursor.

Install The process by which programs and data are copied to the hard drive of a computer system and otherwise prepared for access and use.

Installation agreement A version of the license agreement that appears on the computer screen when software is being installed and prompts the user to accept or decline.

Instant messaging (IM) A private chat in which users can communicate with each other using the computer to type messages in real time.

Integrated circuit (IC) A thin slice of silicon crystal containing microscopic circuit elements, such as transistors, wires, capacitors, and resistors. *Also called* chip, computer chip, and microchip.

Intellectual property Refers to the ownership of certain types of information, ideas, or representations. Includes patents, trademarks, and copyrighted material, such as music, photos, software, books, and films.

Internet The worldwide communication infrastructure made up of connected computer networks using TCP/IP protocol.

Internet forum A Web site where people post comments to discussion threads (topics) which can be read at any time by others who visit the forum.

Internet Service Provider (ISP) A company that maintains Internet computers and telecommunications equipment in order to provide Internet access to businesses, organizations, and individuals.

Internet telephony A set of hardware and software that allows users to make phone-style calls over the Internet, usually without a long-distance charge. *Also called* Voice over IP (VoIP).

Interpreter A program that converts high-level instructions in a computer program into machine language instructions, one instruction at a time.

IP address A unique identifying number assigned to each computer connected to the Internet.

ISP (Internet Service Provider) *See* Internet Service Provider.

Joystick A pointing input device often used in gaming as an alternative to a mouse.

Keyboard An arrangement of letter, number, and special function keys that acts as the primary input device to the computer.

Keyword A word or term used as the basis for a database or Web-page search.

Kilo- A prefix for a thousand.

Kilobit (Kbit or Kb) Approximately 1,000 bits; exactly 1,024 bits.

Kilobyte (KB) Approximately 1,000 bytes; exactly 1,024 bytes.

Label In a worksheet, any text that is used to describe data.

LAN (local area network) An interconnected group of computers and peripherals located within a relatively limited geographic area, such as a home office, building, or campus.

Laptop *See* Notebook computer.

Laptop computer A type of portable computer that is small and light enough to be carried from one location to another. *See* Notebook computer.

Laser mouse A pointing device that uses a laser as the light source to track movement.

Laser printer A printer that uses laser-based technology, similar to that used by photocopiers, to produce text and graphics.

Layout The physical position of each element on a page, in a spreadsheet, slide, or any report from a database.

LCD (liquid crystal display) A type of flat panel computer screen that produces an image by manipulating light within a layer of liquid crystal cells.

LCD screen *See* LCD.

Library In Windows 7, used to organize files and folders on the storage media by containing links to files that are a similar type such as document files or photo files; default libraries in Windows 7 are Documents, Music, Pictures, and Videos.

License agreement A legal contract that defines the ways in which you may use a computer program. For personal computer software, you will find the license on the outside of the package, on a separate card inside the package, on the CD/DVD packaging, or in one of the program files.

Link The fundamental tool for navigating Web pages. Click a text or graphic link to jump to a location in the same Web page, open a different Web page, or go to a different Web site. *Also called* hyperlink.

Linux An operating system that is a derivative of UNIX and available as freeware.

Local application Software that is intended to be installed on a computer's hard drive.

Mac (Macintosh computer) A personal computer platform designed and manufactured by Apple Computer.

Mac OS The operating system software designed for use on Apple Macintosh computers.

Magnetic storage The recording of data onto disks or tape by magnetizing particles of an oxide-based surface coating.

Mailbox Any storage location for email such as the Inbox or Outbox.

Mainframe computer A large, fast, and expensive computer used by businesses or government agencies to provide centralized storage processing and management for large amounts of data.

Malicious software A type of software that can do harm to your computer data, such as viruses, worms, Trojan horses, and spyware. *Also called* malware.

Malware *See* Malicious software.

Mathematical modeling software A category of software that provides tools for solving a wide range of math, science, and engineering problems.

Media player *See* Digital media player.

Mega- Prefix for a million.

Megabit (Mb or Mbit) Approximately 1 million bits; exactly 1,048,576 bits.

Megabyte (MB) Approximately 1 million bytes; exactly 1,048,576 bytes.

Megahertz (MHz) A measure of frequency equivalent to 1 million cycles per second.

Memory The computer circuitry that holds data waiting to be processed, stored, or output.

Memory stick A type of portable solid-state memory card that can store up to 2 TB of storage with very fast data transfer rates.

Microcomputer A category of computer that is built around one processor chip.

Microprocessor *See* Processor.

Microsoft Windows An operating system developed by Microsoft Corporation that provides a graphical interface. Current version is Microsoft Windows 8. Previous versions include Windows 3.1, Windows 95, Windows 98, Windows ME, Windows 2000, Windows XP, Windows NT, Windows Vista, and Windows 7.

Millisecond (ms) A thousandth of a second; used to measure access time, the time it takes a computer to find data on a storage medium and read it.

Mobile app A program such as a game, calendar, stock market tracker, traffic or weather monitor, or news feed designed to run on mobile devices such as smartphones and tablet computers. *Also called* mobile application.

Modem A device that sends and receives data to and from computers over cable, satellite, or telephone lines.

Modifier key The [Ctrl], [Alt], or [Shift] key, in conjunction with another key, when used to expand the repertoire of available commands.

Monitor A display device that forms an image by converting electrical signals from the computer into points of colored light on the screen; usually a computer's primary output device.

Motherboard The main circuit board in a computer that houses chips and other electronic components.

Mouse An input device that allows the user to select and move objects on the screen by moving it on a surface. *Also called* pointing device.

MP3 A file format that provides highly compressed audio files with very little loss of sound quality.

MP3 player Software and/or hardware that plays MP3 music files.

ms *See* Millisecond (ms).

Multi-core processor A single chip containing the circuitry for multiple processors; faster than a processor with a single core.

Multimedia Messaging Service (MMS) Messages sent using a smartphone or mobile device that can include text of up to 140 to 160 characters and include video, audio, and graphics.

Multiple-user license A software license that allows more than one person to use the software; priced per user and allows the allocated number of people to use the software at any time.

Multitasking Provides processor and memory-management services that allow two or more tasks, jobs, or programs to run simultaneously. Most of today's operating systems offer multitasking services.

Nanosecond A unit of time representing 1 billionth of a second.

Native file format A file format that is unique to a program or group of programs and has a unique file extension.

Navigation keypad On a keyboard, the keypad with the Home, End, and arrow keys; used to efficiently move the screen-based insertion point or cursor.

Nested *See* Nested folders.

Nested folders A method of file management whereby folders are created within folders to hold folders as well as files. *Also called* subfolders.

Netbook A type of portable computer that is smaller than a notebook or a laptop computer. Classified as subnotebooks and sometimes referred to as minilaptops, these small computers are scaled-down versions of standard clamshell-style notebook computers.

Network *See* Computer network.

Network card An expansion board mounted inside a computer to allow access to a local area network.

Network-enabled printer A printer that connects directly to the network, rather than to one of the computers on a network.

Notebook computer Small, lightweight, portable computer that can run on batteries. *Also called* laptop or laptop computer.

Numeric data Numbers that represent quantities and can be used in arithmetic operations.

Numeric keypad Calculator-style input device for numbers located toward the right side of a keyboard.

Object code The low-level instructions that result from compiling source code.

Office productivity software Software that integrates word processing, spreadsheet, database, drawing, and presentation capabilities.

OLED (organic light emitting diodes) A technology used on electronic device screens that features a crisp image and a faster response rate than a standard LCD screen; it also uses less power.

Open source software A category of software, such as Linux, that includes its uncompiled source code, which can be modified and distributed by programmers.

Operating system (OS) System software that controls the computer's use of its hardware resources, such as memory and disk storage space.

Optical drive A CD drive, a DVD drive, a Blu-ray Disc (BD) drive, or a combination drive that is usually mounted inside the system unit.

Optical mouse Pointing device that uses an LED light and computer chip to track a light beam as it moves on a surface, such as a desk or mouse pad.

Optical storage A means of recording data as light and dark spots on a CD, DVD, BD, or other optical media.

Organic light emitting diode *See* OLED.

Output The results produced by a computer (for example, reports, graphs, documents, pictures, and music).

Output device A device, such as a monitor or printer, that displays, prints, or transmits the results of processing from the computer memory.

Pages per minute (ppm) A measure of printer speed; most personal or small business printers are rated 15–30 ppm.

Paint software A category of software that provides a set of electronic pens, brushes, and paints for painting images on the screen. *Also called* image editing software.

Password A special set of characters used to restrict access to a computer or network.

Patch Small program or programs designed to correct, secure, or enhance an existing program.

Path A file's location in a file structure. *See* File specification.

PC A microcomputer that uses Windows software and contains an Intel-compatible processor. *See* Personal computer (PC).

Peripheral device A component or equipment, such as a printer or scanner, that expands a computer's input, output, or storage capabilities.

Personal computer (PC) A microcomputer designed for use by an individual user for applications such as Internet browsing, graphics, email, and word processing; PC often used to refer to personal computers running the Windows platform.

Personal finance software A category of software designed to help manage individual finances.

Peta- Prefix for thousand trillion.

Petabyte (PB) Used to identify vast amounts of data; approximately equal to 1,000 terabytes.

PGA (pin-grid array) A common chip design used for processors.

Photo editing software A category of software that provides tools that simplify common photo editing tasks; includes features specially designed to fix poor-quality photos by modifying contrast and brightness, cropping out unwanted objects, and removing red eye.

Photo printer Uses inkjet technology to produce photographic quality images.

Pixel (picture element) The smallest unit in a graphic image. Computer display devices use a matrix of pixels to display text and graphics.

Platform A family or category of computers based on the same underlying software and hardware.

Plug and Play (PnP) The ability of a computer to recognize and adjust the system configuration for a newly added device automatically.

Pointing device An input device, such as a mouse, that you use to manipulate an on-screen pointer and other screen-based graphical controls.

Pointing stick Pointing device typically used with notebook computers as an alternative to a mouse that looks like a pencil eraser and is embedded in the keyboard of a notebook computer. Push up, down, or sideways to move the on-screen pointer. *Also called* TrackPoint.

Portable application Software designed to run from removable storage such as a CD, DVD, or a USB flash drive.

Portable computer A computer that is small and light enough to be carried from one place to another, including notebook computers, laptop computers, netbooks, and tablet computers.

Portable media player *See* Digital media player.

Portable software *See* Portable application.

Ppm *See* Pages per minute.

Presentation software A category of software that provides tools to combine text, graphics, graphs, animation, and sound into a series of electronic slides that can be output on a projector, or as overhead transparencies, paper copies, or 35-millimeter slides.

Printer A peripheral output device that creates hard copy output, including text, photographs, and graphic images.

Printer resolution The density of the ink on the printed page, determines the quality or sharpness of printed images and text.

Processing The manipulation of data (symbols that represent facts, objects, and ideas) using a systematic series of actions.

Processor An integrated circuit that contains the circuitry for processing data. It is a single-chip version of the central processing unit (CPU) found in all computers. *Also called* a microprocessor.

Processor clock A device on the motherboard of a computer responsible for setting the pace of executing instructions.

Productivity software Any type of application software that has the potential to help people do their work more efficiently.

Program The instructions that tell a computer how to perform a specific task such as word processing, graphics, or email. *Also called* application software or software.

Programming language Provides the tools that a programmer uses to create software. *Also called* computer language.

Project management software A category of software specifically designed as a tool for planning, scheduling, and tracking projects and their costs.

Proprietary software Software program that has restrictions on its use that are delineated by copyright, patents, or license agreements. Might be free or distributed commercially and includes commercial software, demoware, shareware, freeware, and open source software.

Public domain software Any software that is available for use by the public without restriction, except that it cannot be copyrighted.

RAM (random access memory) A type of computer memory circuit that holds data, program instructions, and the operating system while the computer is on.

RAM cache Special high-speed memory that gives the CPU rapid access to data that would otherwise be accessed from memory elsewhere on the motherboard. *Also called* cache.

Random access The ability of a storage device (such as a hard drive) to go directly to a specific storage location without having to search sequentially from a beginning location. *Also called* direct access.

Read-only (ROM) technology Data stamped on the CD or DVD surface when it was manufactured, such as commercial software, music, and movies.

Read-write head The mechanism in a hard drive that magnetizes particles on the storage disk surface to write data, or senses the bits that are present to read data.

Record In the context of database management, a record is the set of fields of data that pertain to a single entity in a database.

Recordable technology Optical storage technology used to create CDs, DVDs, and BDs.

Reference software A category of software that provides a collection of information and a way to access that information.

Resolution The density of the grid used to display or print text and graphics, usually expressed in pixels; the greater the horizontal and vertical density, the higher the resolution.

Resource In the context of a computer system, refers to any component that is required to perform work such as the processor, RAM, storage space, and peripherals.

Response rate In the context of display device technology, response rate is how fast a screen updates the information being displayed.

Restore point A snapshot of your computer settings created by a Windows utility either automatically when you install new software, or manually that you can use if you have a hard drive failure or instability.

Rewritable technology (RW) An optical storage technology that uses phase change technology to alter a crystal structure on the disc surface to create patterns of light and dark spots, making it possible for stored data to be recorded and erased or modified multiple times.

ROM (read-only memory) One or more integrated circuits that contain permanent instructions the computer uses during the boot process.

ROM BIOS (basic input/output system) A small set of basic input/output system instructions stored in ROM that causes the computer system to load critical operating files when the user turns on the computer.

Root directory The main directory of a disk or other storage medium.

Router The hardware device that connects to computer and to the Internet.

Scanner An input device that converts a printed page of text or images into a digital format.

Screen size On a display device, the measurement in inches from one corner of the screen diagonally across to the opposite corner.

SDRAM (synchronous dynamic RAM) A type of RAM that synchronizes itself with the CPU, thus enabling it to run at much higher clock speeds than conventional RAM.

Search engine Program that uses keywords to find information on the Internet and return a list of relevant documents.

Search site A Web site that provides a variety of tools to help you find information on the Web based on keyword searches.

Secure Digital (SD) card Solid state storage popular for MP3 and digital imaging storage featuring fast data transfer rates.

Security utility Program that protects and secures the computer. Helps control nuisance ads, intrusion attempts, and spam; also provides file-encryption and antivirus software.

Semiconducting material Materials such as silicon and germanium that are used to make chips. The conductive properties create miniature electronic pathways and components, such as transistors. *Also called* semiconductors.

Sequential access A form of data storage, usually on computer tape, that requires a device to read or write data one record after another, starting at the beginning of the medium.

Server A computer on a network that supplies the network with shared data and storage.

Server operating system Provides communications and routing services that allow computers to share data, programs, and peripheral devices by routing data and programs to each user's local computer, where the actual processing takes place.

Server software The software used by servers to locate and distribute data requested by a network or Internet users.

Service pack A collection of updates, fixes, and/or enhancements to a software program delivered in the form of a single installable package usually distributed over the Internet.

Setup program A program module supplied with a software package for the purpose of installing the software.

Shareware Copyrighted software marketed under a license that allows users to use the software for a trial period and then send in a registration fee if they wish to continue to use it.

Shrink-wrap license A software license usually sealed in an envelope, plastic box, or shrink wrapping that goes into effect as soon as you open the packaging.

Single-user license A license that limits use of the software to only one person at a time.

Site license A software license generally priced at a flat rate and allows software to be used on all computers at a specific location.

Skins utility Used to customize screen-based desktops with screensavers that display clever graphics when the machine is idle.

Slide A component of presentation software that combines text, graphics, graphs, animations, and sound into a series of electronic slides for display on a monitor for a one-on-one presentation or on a computer projection device for group presentations.

Smartphone A handheld digital communications device that usually has many features such as removable storage, email, Web access, voice communications, built-in camera, and GPS.

SMS (Short Message Service) System used to send text messages of 140 to 160 characters or less using your smartphone or mobile device. *See* Text messaging.

Social networking An online networking activity that allows registered members to communicate with others in the network such as LinkedIn, and Facebook.

Software The instructions that tell a computer how to perform tasks, such as system software and application software.

Software license A legal contract that defines the ways in which you may use a computer program. For personal computer software, the license is on the outside of the package, on a separate card inside the package, on the CD packaging, or in one of the program files. *Also called* license agreement.

Software suite A collection of application software sold as a single package.

Software upgrade Improvements or enhancements to existing installed softrware that is available to consumers who already have a software program installed.

Solid-state drive (SSD) A storage device that can be internal or external to a computer that has no moving parts.

Solid-state storage A variety of compact storage cards, pens, drives, and sticks that stores data in a nonvolatile, erasable, low-power chip in a microscopic grid of cells.

Solid-state technology Data storage technology that stores data in a durable, erasable, low-power chip with no moving parts.

Sound card A small circuit board that gives the computer the ability to accept audio input from a microphone, play sound files stored on disks and CD-ROMs, and produce audio output through speakers or headphones. Required for high-quality music, narration, and sound effects.

Sound system Speakers and a circuit board (sound card) used to create high-quality music, narration, and sound effects using a computer.

Source code Computer instructions written in a high-level language.

Spam Unwanted electronic junk mail that arrives in your Inbox.

Spam filter Software that automatically routes advertisements and other junk mail to the Deleted Items folder maintained by your email client; can be effective for blocking unwanted emails.

Speakers Output devices that receive signals for the computer's sound card to play music, narration, or sound effects.

Spreadsheet An electronic worksheet for numerical calculations presented in the form of a grid of columns and rows. Each cell in the grid has a unique cell reference, or address, that is based on its column and row location. *Also called* worksheet.

Spreadsheet software The software for creating electronic worksheets that hold data in cells and perform calculations based on that data.

Statistical software A category of software that helps you analyze large sets of data to discover relationships and patterns, summarize survey results, test scores, experiment results, or population data.

Storage The area in a computer that holds data on a permanent basis when it is not immediately needed for processing.

Storage capacity The amount of data that can be stored on a storage medium.

Storage device A mechanical apparatus that records data to and retrieves data from a storage medium.

Storage medium The physical material used to store computer data, such as a flash drive, a hard drive, USB flash drive, or an optical disc.

Storage technology Defines the data storage systems (storage media and storage devices) used by computers to store data and program files.

Stored program A set of instructions that resides on a storage device, such as a hard drive, and can be loaded into memory and executed.

Subdirectory A directory found under the root directory.

Subfolder A method of file management whereby folders are created within folder to hold folders. *Also called* nested folders.

Supercomputer The fastest and most expensive type of computer. At the time it is built, one of the fastest computers in the world; can tackle tasks, such as breaking codes and modeling worldwide weather systems, that would not be practical for other computers.

Swap file The data on the hard drive that has been moved from RAM to virtual memory.

System requirements Specifications for the operating system and hardware configuration necessary for a software product to work correctly.

System software Computer programs that help the computer carry out essential operating tasks, such as an operating system.

System unit The case or box that contains the computer's power supply, storage devices, main circuit board, processor, and memory.

Table (database) An arrangement of data in a grid of rows and columns. In a relational database, a collection of record types with their data.

Table (layout) Gridlike structure that can hold text or pictures.

Tablet computer A portable computing device featuring a touch-sensitive screen that can be used as a writing or a drawing pad.

Tape cartridge A removable magnetic tape module similar to a cassette tape.

Tape storage A sequential magnetic storage technology that consists of a tape for the storage medium and a tape drive for the storage device. Data is arranged as a long sequence of bits that begins at one end of the tape and stretches to the other end.

Tax preparation software A specialized type of personal finance software designed to help gather annual income and expense data, identify deductions, and calculate tax payments.

TCP/IP (Transmission Control Protocol/Internet Protocol) A standard set of communication rules used by every computer that connects to the Internet.

Tera- Prefix for a trillion.

Terabyte Used to identify a large amount of data; approximately equal to a trillion bytes.

Text messaging A system used to send messages of 140 to 160 characters or less using your smartphone, or mobile device. *See* SMS (Short Message Service).

Toner The fine powder in the cartridges used in laser printers that creates the image on the page.

Touch screen technology Display device technology that makes it possible for a single touch or handwriting to be used to input data.

Touchpad An alternative input device often found on notebook computers. *Also called* trackpad.

Trackball Pointing input device used as an alternative to a mouse.

Trackpad An alternative input device often found on notebook computers. *Also called* touchpad.

Tracks A series of concentric or spiral storage areas created on a storage medium during the formatting process.

Unicode A 16-bit character representation code that can represent more than 65,000 characters.

Uninstall To remove software files, references, and Windows Registry entries from a computer's hard drive.

UNIX A multi-user, multitasking server operating system developed by AT&T's Bell Laboratories in 1969.

Unzipped Refers to files that have been uncompressed.

Uploading The process of sending a copy of a file from a local computer to a remote computer.

URL (Uniform Resource Locator) The unique address of a Web page.

USB drive *See* USB flash drive.

USB flash drive A portable solid state storage device featuring a built-in connector that plugs directly into a computer's USB port. *Also called* USB drive.

USB (universal serial bus) port Popular ports for connecting peripheral devices including mice, cameras, mp3 players, scanners, and printers that have USB connections.

User ID A combination of letters and numbers that identifies a user on a computer. *Also called* a username.

User interface The software and hardware that enable people to interact with computers.

Username *See* User ID.

Utility software A subcategory of system software designed to augment the operating system by providing ways for a user to control the allocation and use of hardware resources. *Also called* utilities.

Validation code Series of alphanumeric characters supplied by the software publisher that is required to complete the installation of software.

Value A number used in a calculation.

Video card *See* Graphics card.

Video editing software Category of software that provides a set of tools for transferring video footage from a digital video camera to a computer, clipping out unwanted footage, assembling video segments in any sequence, adding special visual effects, and adding a sound track.

Viewing angle width Measurement of a monitor or display device that indicates how far to the side you can still clearly see the screen image.

Virtual memory A computer's use of hard drive storage to simulate RAM.

Voice Over IP (VOIP) Technology used to send and receive voice conversations over the Internet. *Also called* Internet telephony.

Volatile Data that can exist only with a constant power supply.

Web (World Wide Web) An Internet service that links documents and information from computers distributed all over the world using the HTTP protocol.

Web application (Web app) Software that, instead of being installed on a local computer, is accessed with a Web browser; runs on a remote computer connected to the Internet.

Web authoring software Category of software that provides easy-to-use tools for composing, assembling, and generating HTML to develop Web pages.

Web-based email An email account that stores, sends, and receives email on a Web site rather than a program on a user's computer.

Web browser A program such as Internet Explorer, Firefox, or Safari that communicates with a Web server and displays Web pages.

Web cam A camera that captures digital video images using a computer.

Web page A document on the World Wide Web that consists of a specially coded HTML file with associated text, audio, video, graphics, and links to other Web pages.

Web server A computer and software that stores and transmits Web pages to computers connected to the Internet.

Web site Location on the World Wide Web that contains information stored in Web pages relating to specific topics.

Widget Term used to define a utility program on an Apple computer's desktop used to display information such as a clock, calendar, calculator, news aggregators, notes, and weather.

Wiki A collaborative Web site that allows people to add to and modify material posted by others.

Windows *See* Microsoft Windows.

Windows Explorer A file management utility included with most Windows operating systems that helps users manage their files.

Windows Phone A version of the Windows operating system designed for portable or mobile computers and smartphones.

Windows Registry A crucial data file maintained by the Windows operating system that contains the settings for hardware and software that has been installed on the system. *Also called* Registry.

Word processing software A category of software that assists the user in producing documents, such as reports, letters, papers, and manuscripts.

Word size The number of bits a CPU can manipulate at one time, which is dependent on the size of the registers in the CPU and the number of data lines in the bus.

Worksheet A computerized, or electronic, spreadsheet, based on a grid of columns and rows.

Workstation (1) A computer connected to a local area network. (2) A powerful desktop computer designed for specific tasks.

Zeta- Prefix for sextillion.

Zettabyte Used to identify vast amounts of data; approximately equal to 1,000 exabytes (2^{70} bytes).

Index